ORCAGNA'S TABERNACLE

IN ORSANMICHELE,

FLORENCE

ORCAGNA'S TABERNACLE

IN ORSANMICHELE,

FLORENCE

BY GERT KREYTENBERG

PHOTOGRAPHS BY DAVID FINN

HARRY N. ABRAMS, INC., PUBLISHERS

HALF TITLE:
Orcagna's tabernacle, in the northeastern corner of the oratory.

FRONTISPIECE:
Head of the Theological Virtue
Caritas (Love or Charity), from
the south socle.

OPPOSITE:
Inlay work on the spiral colonnettes of the piers.

OVERLEAF:
(Left) Relief of *Caritas*, from
the south socle; *(right)* trumpet-
playing angel from the *Assumption of the Virgin* relief on the
east wall .

CONTENTS PAGE:
(Left) Angel carrying the mandorla of the Virgin, from the
Assumption of the Virgin relief
on the east wall; *(right)* lion
guarding the base of an inlaid
colonnette at a corner of the
balustrade.

Editor: Elaine M. Stainton
Designers: Samuel N. Antupit and Maria L. Miller
Translated from the German by Gerald Williams

Library of Congress Cataloging-in-Publication Data

Kreytenberg, Gert.
Orcagna's tabernacle in Orsanmichele, Florence /
by Gert Kreytenberg ; photographs by David Finn.
p.   cm.
Includes bibliographical references and index.
ISBN 0–8109–3675–5
1. Orcagna, fl. 1343–1368. Tabernacle. 2. Orcagna, fl.
1343–1368—Criticism and interpretation. 3. Mary,
Blessed Virgin, Saint—Art. 4. Orsanmichele
(Church : Florence, Italy)
I. Orcagna, fl. 1343–1368. II. Finn, David 1921–
III. Title.
NB623.O73A76   1994
726'.5291—dc20   94–2870

Published in 1994 by Harry N. Abrams, Incorporated,
New York
A Times Mirror Company

Printed and bound in Japan

CONTENTS

Above: Detail of the *Annunciation*, from the west socle.

Right: Head of the Virtue *Virginitas* (Virginity), from the southeastern corner pier.

Left: Detail of a prophet, from the southwestern corner pier.

Above: Head of the Cardinal Virtue *Justitia*, from the northwestern corner pier.

Above: Man with tendrils growing from his body, from the base of the *Death and Assumption of the Virgin* relief on the east wall.

Right: Detail of painted glass decoration.

Left: The Apostle Peter, from the southwestern corner pier, displaying the opening of the Apostles' Creed: *Credo in Deum patrem omnipotentem, creatorem caeli et terrae.*

Above: Head of the Cardinal Virtue *Temperantia* (Temperance), from the southeastern corner pier.

PHOTOGRAPHER'S NOTE

During the course of the last several decades I have photographed many masterpieces of Renaissance sculpture for books on the great artists of the period.

Donatello, whose profoundly moving insights into the human condition were a revelation to me, was the first to show me how my camera could translate three-dimensional works of art into striking two-dimensional images. Andrea Pisano and Lorenzo Ghiberti taught me how to use my close-up lenses to discover the beauty of the jewel-like surfaces and wonderfully inventive figures on the doors of the Florentine Baptistry. The unequaled mastery of Michelangelo, seen in the smallest bozzetti as well as his most monumental carvings, provided an inexhaustible source of inspiration. The classical splendor of Cellini, the rhythmic harmonies of Giambologna, the astonishing virtuosity of Bernini—all provided their own special visual qualities which I attempted to capture photographically.

Although I did not originally expect to include the work of Andrea Orcagna in this august company, I always paid a visit to the church of Orsanmichele whenever I was in Florence. Remarkable as the sculptures in the niches outside the building are, it was the interior that always proved to be the crowning point of my visit. I loved the great architectural space and the glorious decoration on the vaults and ceiling, and I thought that Orcagna's tabernacle was one of the most marvelous creations I had ever seen. When I put a coin in the light box, it was possible for a brief moment to be dazzled by what was there, but the spotlights tended to flatten out the forms; I could do little more than glimpse something very grand, very complex, very intricate. Then on one visit I made up my mind to find a way to explore the work photographically.

Getting permission in Florence to photograph any important work is a challenge, and for a variety of reasons. Orcagna's tabernacle proved to be especially difficult. It took some time to find out which authorities needed to give their approval, but eventually I took all the necessary steps and received clearance. The final permission had to come from the priest of the church, and after all the others had agreed, it took some persuading to get his approval as well. In time the priest became my friend, and today we greet each other enthusiastically whenever we meet, but at the beginning he was very skeptical about an intruder in his church, running wires for lights across the floor to a distant outlet (about thirty feet away from the tabernacle), creating a hazard for tourists who crowd into the church in large groups, and being a general nuisance.

I still remember the first time I opened the gate in the iron railing to crawl into the narrow space surrounding the tabernacle. I felt as if I were entering an inner sanctum; outside the railing it was dark, and I could barely see the people milling around. I forgot all about them when I set up my lights and began to examine the sculptures now only a few inches away from my eye.

Opposite: Head of the Theological Virtue *Fides* (Faith), from the north socle.

I had never imagined that anything so breathtaking existed. The details of the faces and figures, the colors and patterns of the glass, the harmony of the design of every part—all were extraordinary. I had to maneuver my lights carefully in the cramped spaces to bring out the forms of the reliefs, but when I managed to do so and saw the results in my test Polaroid shots, I was thrilled. This was going to be one of the great photographic adventures of my life.

I knew the project would take years to complete, but I wanted to do it right. And so every few months I made my pilgrimage to Florence, took hundreds of photographs, and spent days in the darkroom making prints back at home, enjoying the sense of working on a project that I had come to think would be of historic importance.

I had no idea whether a publisher would be interested in the project, or if any one of the art historians I knew might be willing to write a text. That would come later. My goal was to produce a collection of photographs that would show the details of the tabernacle as they had never been seen before. The rest would follow.

Making prints of my photographs, both color and black-and-white, was as exciting to me as shooting them. As I saw one spellbinding shot after another appear on paper, I couldn't resist making some large prints for my office. The most striking of these were a series of large, 20"x 24" prints of the small faces of the relief figures around the base. The faces themselves were less than 2" high, but when they were enlarged they had a mesmerizing power. One day Paul Gottlieb, the president of Harry N. Abrams, Inc., was in my office and saw the large prints. He was overwhelmed. When I told him about the tabernacle, he said, "We must do a book on it!" That was how I found my publisher.

Subsequently I asked the advice of John Pope-Hennessy, with whom I had worked on a book on the sculpture of Cellini, whether he could recommend an author. Without any hesitation, he suggested Gert Kreytenberg, a scholar who was then working at I Tatti, Bernard Berenson's villa and library in Settignano, just outside of Florence, now a Harvard University study center. Dr. Kreytenberg had written extensively on the artists of the fourteenth century, and would be an ideal choice for the Orcagna project. I arranged to meet him in the I Tatti library to discuss the project. He was delighted to see some of my photographs and was enthusiastic about writing the text for what he believed would be an important book. Not long after, Harry N. Abrams, Inc. signed a contract with him and he began to write the manuscript.

After I had finished photographing the sculptures at eye level, I had to figure out how to reach the sculpture higher up on the tabernacle. Obviously I would need a scaffold. Long negotiations were required to make the necessary arrangements and to persuade the authorities and the priest to let me set it up. Eventually I succeeded.

The sculptures seen from on high were as magnificent as those below, although lighting them was far more difficult. When photographing sculpture it is generally important to have the light come from above. That is how one can project the right shadow on the face —to show the indentation of the eyes, bring out the forms of the cheeks, highlight the nose, the lips, the chin, and so on. Sculptors tend to work with light from above, whether they do so outdoors or in a studio, and that is the way their forms can be seen best. While photographing on the scaffold, it was impossible to place a light above the sculpture, so I had to be satisfied with lighting that was not ideal. My worst problem at the top of the tabernacle, however, was not light but dust. There seemed to be centuries of accumulated dust and cobwebs on the tops of the figures, which I couldn't reach with a brush or cloth. Some of the photographs of these sculptures were so poor as to be unusable, but there were many that turned out beautifully, particularly the details on the relief of the *Death of the Virgin* on the back of the tabernacle.

When I was finished I felt I had done justice to one of the most beautiful works ever produced by human hands. The adventure had been an exciting part of my life for so long I was a little sad that it was over. But I felt that with Gert Kreytenberg's excellent text, our book would help Orcagna's tabernacle in Orsanmichele receive the recognition it deserved as one of the great wonders in the history of art.

David Finn

FOREWORD

In the fourteenth century, the image of the Madonna in the church of Orsanmichele was one of the most important sites of the cult of the Virgin in Florence. As time went on, its importance grew, owing to a number of miraculous cures that were attributed to it. The cult was fostered by a lay society, the *Compagnia della Madonna di Orsanmichele*, whose members were called *Laudesi* because of their pledge to participate in worshipping the image. In the middle of the century, the *Laudesi's* wealth and religious zeal led them to commission the painter Andrea di Cione, called Orcagna, to replace the tabernacle which held the miraculous image with a new, monumental shrine of extraordinary size and magnificence. The sheer opulence of this new tabernacle, which resembles a gigantic goldsmith's work, even today impresses the spectator as an intimation of heavenly splendor.

Surprisingly, Orcagna's tabernacle has remained largely unknown. Few photographs of its 117 reliefs and statues have ever been published. Of the thirty-six sculptures on its socle and rear wall, only ten scenes from the Life of Mary have been reproduced; the few photographs of the remaining sculptures that have been published give only a general view of the artist's work. The quality of their printing has been good enough for iconographic study, but not for a critical examination that addresses questions of attribution and stylistic development.

David Finn's photographs here reproduce all thirty-six sculptures on the socle and on the back wall of the tabernacle in proper context for the first time. More importantly, they make it possible to view these works in depth, bringing details of their extraordinary artistic quality into focus.

I would like to express my gratitude to: Signora Pelliconi (Soprintendenza per i Beni Artistici e Storici, Florence), Dott.ssa P. Grifoni and Dott.ssa F. Nanelli (Soprintendenza ai Monumenti, Florence), and Don Pilade Filippini, in whose custody Orsanmichele currently resides, for permission to reproduce these photographs of the tabernacle's sculptures. Special thanks are due to my colleagues and friends, Dott. Giorgio Bonsanti and Dott. Bruno Santi. I also wish to thank Prof. G. De Juliis, for informative talks about Orcagna's tabernacle throughout the years, and Prof. G. Rocchi, for his information regarding the work of his students, C. Pisetta and G. Vitali. Without the Kunsthistorisches Institut in Florence, and the Harvard Center for Italian Renaissance Studies at the Villa I Tatti, which generously enabled me to proceed with my Orcagna studies through a fellowship in 1987/88, this book could not have been written. I am deeply indebted to both institutions.

Opposite: Detail of the Cardinal Virtue *Fortitudo* (Fortitude), from the southwestern corner pier *(see plates 80–81).*

Gert Kreytenberg
Dorsten, Germany, May 1991

I

ORSANMICHELE

PURPOSE, LOCATION, STRUCTURE

The church of Orsanmichele in Florence is a structure unique in the world. Outwardly, it resembles a palace. Its interior, however, is surprisingly simple. It has three floors, each of which consists of a single large room. Until the middle of the fourteenth century, the first floor was an open loggia, used as a marketplace for grain merchants to conduct their trade. The second and third floors, accessible by a staircase in the northwestern corner pillar, housed the municipal granary; from there grain could be sent down to the market through chutes set in two pillars along the north wall. In 1361, however, the market was moved elsewhere, and the first floor of the building was converted to an oratory for the veneration of the Virgin.

The tabernacle, with its miraculous image of the Madonna, stands at the east side of the hall, where Orsanmichele borders the Via dei Calzaiuoli. This street directly unites the cathedral and baptistry—the religious center of the city—with the Palazzo dei Priori (Palazzo Vecchio), the political center and seat of government.

Also on the Via dei Calzaiuoli are the Church of San Carlo dei Lombardi, opposite the east side of Orsanmichele, and the houses of two powerful religious confraternities: on the south side, the *Compagnia della Madonna di Orsanmichele*, which was responsible for the care of the miraculous image; and on the north side, the *Compagnia del Bigallo*, which cared for the sick. Nearby are the palaces of the *Arte dei Beccai* (the butchers' guild) on Orsanmichele's north side, and the *Arte della Lana* (the wool weavers' guild) on its west side; unfortunately, the *Arte dei Chiavaioli* (the locksmiths' guild), which stood on the south side, is now gone. These palaces housed three of the twenty-one guilds which, in the fourteenth century, elected the government of the Florentine Republic. Thus the grain market, with its miraculous image, stood prominently amid a number of distinguished buildings, its unusual height enhancing its significance to the Florentine people. Indeed, the structure might almost be considered the city's epicenter; with honored religious foundations to its east, and important political and commercial buildings to its west, it stood at the center of Florence's secular and sacred spheres, whose coexistence epitomized life in the city in the late Middle Ages.

The unknown architect of Orsanmichele—possibly the painter and sculptor Maso di Banco—designed a tall and narrow rectangular structure. In order to visualize it as the architect originally planned it, we must imagine the first floor as it was in the fourteenth century: an open loggia supporting a two-story granary. This is Orsanmichele as it was originally conceived. The requirement of a market hall, granary, and palace on one site was a novelty in European architecture; there was no example for the architect to follow. The commission must have been devised by the city's leading merchants and politicians, who, in Florence at that time, were the same. One factor that made this unusual commission possible was that no consideration had to be given to neighboring buildings; Orsanmichele, surrounded on all sides by streets, is completely free-standing.

The narrow, rectangular structure was built of smooth blocks of ocher sandstone (*macigno*), whose form and surface give the walls an air of plastic substantiality made all the more emphatic by Orsanmichele's physical independence.

The articulation of the building's façades expresses its interior layout; thus, the arrangement of the three floors is marked on the outer walls by rows of arcades and windows. Likewise, projecting mouldings demarcate the height of the floors, each of which is composed of six bays. The building's long sides have three arcades and three windows; the short sides have two of each.

Today the arcades of the first floor are closed off, so that the entire rectangular contour of the building rests on the ground. When the arcades were still open, the main body of the building stood on massive piers.

Today the exterior piers are fused with the outer surface of the building; at the corners, these supports are somewhat broader than are those in between. Each pier has a moulding that sets off its base from its shaft. Above this is a second, slightly less pronounced moulding, and above that, a niche which fills most of the upper part of the pier. (Inside the building, on the narrow interior face of each pillar, is a pilaster, marked by a shallow recess.) Each pier is crowned by a third moulding with a cornice frieze, from which spring the round arches of the arcades. Slightly above the top of the arcades is a fourth moulding, which runs completely around the building. Set into the exterior wall, in the spandrels between the arches and the mouldings that separate the first and second floors, are tondi. The three floors are uniformly set off from each other by a moulding. Above the axes of the arcades are huge, open lancet windows with tracery. The walls of both upper floors, which are analogous to the first floor, have mouldings which subdivide the walls at the springing of the arches. Finally, a broad, projecting cornice crowns the entire building, masking the proportionally low height of the roof.

The building's proportions and the systemization of its vocabulary are complex. For example, the ratio of the widths to the lengths of both the arcades and the windows are 2:3. There is, however, one irregularity: the pillars on the west side, owing to the steps in the northwestern corner pillar, are somewhat larger than those at the east side of the building. The heights of the three floors diminish as they ascend. The upper and lower sections of the first floor are of equal height. On the second floor, the lower section is considerably shorter than the one above it. On the third floor, the sections (not including the cornices) are again of equal height. The irregularity of the middle floor is puzzling, until one sees that the lower, shorter section is the same height as each of the two sections of the upper floor, while the longer upper section is as high as those of the first floor. In effect, the sections of the second floor are interrelated with the adjacent sections on the upper and lower floors. Thus, the top section of the first floor and the adjacent lower section of the second floor correspond in size to the top section of the second floor and the adjacent lower section of the top floor. In this way the division of the walls of Orsanmichele is carried through the three floors, each section interconnected with another.

The design of Orsanmichele—especially its interior—is strongly reminiscent of the Palazzo dei Priori. But no building in Florence shows a similar balance of proportions, or a like harmony of forms.

The monastery of San Michele in Orto (St. Michael in the Garden) formerly stood on the present site of Orsanmichele, its memory surviving in the oratory's name. The monastery was probably destroyed in 1239 during one of Florence's numerous factional wars. The municipal government took control of the empty lot, which seemed suitable for a public square, and in 1285, allowed an open marketplace for grain to be constructed on it. In 1291 a confraternity (the *Compagnia dei Laudesi della Madonna di Orsanmichele*) was established for the veneration of the Madonna of Orsanmichele, a painting attached to one of the pilasters in the market hall. According to the chronicler Giovanni Villani, this image of the Madonna began to perform miracles in 1292, curing the sick and the lame, and exorcising devils from the possessed. As a result, the Madonna became the focus of an important Florentine cult.

In 1304, the grain market was destroyed by a fire, which may also have consumed the miraculous painting; there is no indication, however, that the cult was disbanded. A new building was constructed in 1307/8, evidently not as sound as its predecessor, for it needed repairs in 1321 and 1332.

In 1336, the municipality concluded that the building was not large enough to store the public grain supply properly, and that it was a reproach to the city. They therefore decided to build a new grain hall in the form of a palace, large enough to house both the municipal grain supply and the cult of the miracle-working Madonna.

A committee was set up to prepare for the new construction. It was decided that two floors would be built above the market hall to serve as granaries. On July 29, 1337, the foundation stone was laid; the construction, which was supervised by the *Arte della Seta* (silk guild), proceeded at a slow pace. When in 1339 it was announced that the guilds could have statues of their patron saints adorning the exterior niches of the building's piers, only the three most powerful guilds began to work on the project.

A new cult of St. Anne was established in Orsanmichele to commemorate the saint's Feast Day in 1343, when Walter of Brienne, the so-called Duke of Athens, was expelled from Florence after eleven months of tyrannical rule. The new cult, however, did not accelerate the progress of the work.

By 1350, the piers and exterior walls of the hall had been built, but none of the six bays were yet vaulted. When in 1352, Orcagna began working on the tabernacle for the miraculous image of the Madonna, the vault of the southeastern bay, where the shrine was to stand, was probably the only one completed. The other five were certainly completed by 1357, when the grain market hall was declared finished.

In the summer of 1360, Orcagna concluded his work on the tabernacle (although it is dated 1359). Perhaps the magnificence of the shrine was one reason that the building was soon after devoted entirely to religious use. In any case, the grain market was moved from Orsanmichele in 1361.

During 1366/67 and 1378/80, the open arcades of the market hall were filled in with tracery paneling. At first, these were not installed in the two arches on the west wall, nor in the adjacent or middle arches on the north wall, apparently to permit easy access to the granaries through the stairs in the northwestern corner pier. The arches near the tabernacle itself were filled in first, followed by those at the south and east sides, and one on the north side.

Artist's conception of Orsanmichele as it was in the fourteenth century. The first floor was an open loggia, used as a grain market. Municipal granaries occupied the second and third floors.

Then, around 1380, it was decided that stained-glass windows should be set in the upper part of the tracery, and the arcades closed off. The middle sections of the arcade windows were left open, however, until 1770.

In the late fourteenth century, small reliefs of the Apostles, Evangelists and Virtues, originally commissioned from the sculptor Giovanni di Balduccio for the second tabernacle of the miraculous image of the Madonna, were affixed to the exterior walls of the filled-in arcades.

Between roughly 1369 and 1380, the granaries were built. The marble trim for the upper floor windows was probably finished in 1380, at which time the roof was already under construction. The building was completed in 1404, when the cornices were installed on the top floor.

THE VARIOUS MADONNA PAINTINGS AND TABERNACLES

The image housed in Orcagna's shrine was painted by Bernardo Daddi in 1347. This panel is the last of probably three consecutive versions of the Madonna of Orsanmichele.

25

According to the chronicler Villani, a Madonna image on one of the pilasters in the loggia began performing miracles on July 3, 1292; his text does not say whether this was a panel painting or a fresco. The *Capitoli della Compagnia della Madonna di Orsanmichele* of 1294, the first statute of the confraternity, is also silent on this point, but it does mention a panel painting of the archangel Michael displayed nearby, which suggests that the Madonna may also have been on a panel. The statute also makes plain that the image of the Madonna was kept piously covered by a curtain, which could be raised and lowered. The painting was unveiled at specific times by the cult of the *Laudesi*, but could also be shown by one of the confraternity's directors (*capitani*), the provost (*preposto*), or the treasurer at the request of devout visitors. The statute required that two large candles be lit while the image was displayed.

It is not known for certain whether the panels of the Madonna and St. Michael were destroyed during the terrible fire of June 10, 1304, which devastated the entire district, but it would seem likely that they were. The confraternity probably continued to function and to maintain the cult while the burned-out grain market was repaired; probably a new image was commissioned immediately after the catastrophe. This second Madonna is now lost. Attempts to identify various Madonna panels in or near Florence as this second miraculous image are not convincing; they are replicas of it, as is a fresco of the Madonna in the chapter room of the guild hall of the wool weavers, across the street from Orsanmichele. In spite of the poor preservation of the throne in this painting, it is clear from the poses of Mary and the child, and from the arrangement of the eight angels around them—the lower one holding a censer—that they replicate exactly the composition of Bernardo Daddi's 1347 panel in Orcagna's tabernacle. This guild hall fresco may date from 1310/20 or 1342/47, but in any case, it predates Daddi's panel. Their similarities can be explained only by direct reference to the now lost second Madonna of Orsanmichele. Thus, Daddi's 1347 version closely resembles the Madonna painted directly after the 1304 fire, which was itself certainly modeled on the original image, in order to encourage continuity of the cult.

We can see reflections of the second Madonna image in three different manuscript illustrations from around 1340, although these miniatures, according to the custom of the time, do not copy it exactly. In the first of these, a decorated initial on the front page of the *Libro dei Lasciti alla Compagnia dei Capitani di Orsanmichele*, a register of bequests to the confraternity from 1340 to 1347, a certain "Master of the Dominican Effigies" painted the enthroned Madonna surrounded by angels. The second example, in Giovanni Villani's *Nuova Cronica* of 1340/48 [Folio 152r (Rome, Bibl. Vat.) Cod. Chigi L. VII. 296], depicts the miraculous image of Orsanmichele somewhat simply, but clearly shows that the second Madonna was framed by architecture. This architectural frame is represented in meticulous detail in a third manuscript, the *Specchio Umano* of 1335/40, by the grain merchant Domenico Lenzi [Folio 79r (Florence, Bibl. Laur.) Ms Tempi 3]. Here one recognizes a tabernacle which already corresponds to the one which Orcagna was later commissioned to build. It clearly has a quadratic ground plan, a fenced-in socle area, possibly with a gate at the rear, and an arch standing on each of the four sides of the socle, with pilasters at the corners. The rear arch frames the miraculous image, and the interior of the shrine seems to be vaulted. The corner pilasters end in pinnacles, and gables rise over the arches. Towering above the vault is a steep, pyramidal canopy, whose ribs are decorated with crockets.

This detailed drawing of the tabernacle corresponds exactly with its description in the *Capitoli della Compagnia della Madonna di Orsanmichele* of August 10, 1333. Rubric X describes the duties of the confraternity's staff, which cared for the miraculous image day and night. These men accepted offerings, lit the lamps around the tabernacle (here referred to as the oratory), and remained in constant attendance. During the day, one of their number had to remain inside the tabernacle precinct, not leaving unless relieved by another. The gate was always kept locked.

Rubric XXX reveals that the painting of the Madonna was protected by one or more fine silk veils. On Sundays and holidays it was put on display, as it was when a sermon was delivered in the hall. Whenever the painting was unveiled, the two large candles in front of it had to be lit. Devout visitors could view it for a short period of time only by authorization from one of the *capitani* or the *preposto*.

The tabernacle described in this statute was plainly a monumental architectural work, and its depiction in the *Specchio Umano* (1335/40) shows that it had already been built. Its sculptor was the same Giovanni di Balduccio mentioned earlier, whose reliefs of the Apostles, Evangelists, and Virtues would later be affixed to the exterior partition walls of Orsanmichele's arcades.

Giovanni di Balduccio's reliefs, judging from their style, probably date from around 1333, and were certainly created for the then-existing market hall. In that loggia however, a cycle of the apostles and the virtues could only have been intended for the tabernacle of the miraculous image of the Madonna. Significantly, Orcagna's shrine also includes these two cycles. Four apostle reliefs by Giovanni di Balduccio may have occupied three sides of the socle, while the four reliefs of virtues (two of which are in the Museo Nazionale del Bargello in Florence, and in the National Gallery of Art in Washington) were probably set at its corners. The two evangelist reliefs were probably located by the small gate at the rear. Finally, a relief of Christ in a mandorla, now in the Museo Arqueologico Nacional, Madrid, which has been traditionally referred to as the "axial of the Madonna of the Miraculous Image," probably adorned the gable over the front arcade.

In short, Giovanni di Balduccio's tabernacle and the one defined in the 1333 *Capitoli* match each other exactly.

We know from the *Capitoli* of 1294 and 1297 that in the first grain market loggia (1285–1304), there was a device that enabled the miracle-working Madonna on the pilaster to be veiled and unveiled. After the fire of 1304, the first Madonna was quickly replaced by a second one. Whether this second Madonna was equipped with a similar veiling mechanism is unknown. By 1333, as we know from the *Capitoli*, the surviving sculptures, and the manuscript illustrations, a tabernacle—Giovanni di Balduccio's—housed the second miraculous image. This tabernacle was the example that Orcagna would be obliged to follow in creating his own.

II

THE PATRON AND THE ARTIST OF
THE EXISTING TABERNACLE

THE COMPAGNIA DELLA MADONNA DI ORSANMICHELE

In the preamble of the 1294 *Capitoli della Compagnia della Madonna di Orsanmichele*, the foundation day of the brotherhood is given as August 10, 1291. Its chief task was the veneration of the Madonna, and also, in the beginning, of an image of St. Michael, which was on another pilaster in the loggia of the grain market. The confraternity members sang praises (*laudi*) before the venerated images, hence their name *Laudesi*. They were also obliged to contribute to the public welfare by giving alms to the poor, to religious orders, and to hospitals. In these obligations, the *Laudesi* were similar to other lay brotherhoods, the earliest of which were established in 1244 by the Dominican saint Peter Martyr. These were the *Compagnia del Bigallo* and the *Compagnia di Laudi di Santa Maria Novella*. Other similar organizations followed. The *Compagnia di Santa Maria del Carmine* was begun in 1248; the *Compagnia di Santa Reparata* in 1281; and the *Compagnia di Laudi di Santa Croce* in 1290. Unlike other lay brotherhoods, which were attached to specific churches and founded by corresponding monks or by a bishop, the confraternity of Orsanmichele came into existence through the spontaneous veneration of the Madonna by the laity.

According to Villani, the painting began performing miracles (*gradi e aperti miracoli*) on July 3, 1292: *sanado infermi, e rizzando attritti, e isgombrare imperversati visibilmente in grande quantita*. People flocked to the image in great numbers, which aroused envy among the Dominicans and Franciscans, who disputed the miracles' authenticity. Presumably for that reason the *Compagnia* had to wait until 1294 for the approval of the bishop to obtain its charter.

According to the *Capitoli* of 1294, the enterprise was overseen by six *capitani* (directors), three treasurers for the management of debts and property; a notary to keep account of revenues and expenditures; twelve advisors; four *ammonitori* to look after the needs of the members; four instructors for the rehearsal of hymns; three sextons and two clerks, who received the offerings made to the image. With the exception of the clerks, the sextons and the notary, all of these offices were honorary. The *capitani* were elected from the *consiglio generale* upon the recommendation of their predecessors for a term of four months. Each *capitano* served as the main *preposto* for twenty days.

Any man could become a member of the *Compagnia*. A prospective brother had to be enrolled by a notary and then pay a monthly fee of two *denari*. As a member, he was obliged to say five Our Fathers and five Hail Marys daily; twelve more were required when another member of the *Compagnia* died. Every Sunday afternoon, and daily during Lent, the brotherhood heard a sermon in honor of the Virgin given in front of the miraculous image by a qualified preacher. Brothers were required to confess at least twice a year.

Opposite: Detail of Orcagna's Strozzi altarpiece in Santa Maria Novella, showing Mary as the sponsor of St. Thomas Aquinas.

The welfare of the souls of deceased members had a particular significance. On Mondays, the *capitani* had to see to it that six masses were said for the deceased, one in each *sesto* (municipal district). Every Wednesday morning, and again on Thursday, they had mass celebrated in a different church, so that in time all of the churches were visited. It was also the *capitani's* responsibility to see to it that *laudi* (hymns) were sung for dead members on the eve of every Feast of Mary, and on thirteen other holidays. When a member died, the brotherhood provided the pall, two large candles, and the pillow. A vigil was held in the decedent's parish church; for this purpose, the treasurer provided twelve *denari* and six candles.

The statutes disclose that the Madonna was kept behind a curtain, which could be raised or lowered. The image was revealed whenever *laudi* were sung in the evening, and also for mass and for sermons.

According to the statutes of 1294, the *capitani* were obliged, during the first eight days of their duty, to assemble their counselors and report to them on the distribution of alms.

It is remarkable that the brotherhood, although primarily religious in nature, in no way submitted to any ecclesiastical authority; it was purely a lay confraternity. The first statutes were somewhat expanded in 1297, 1329, and 1333, however, they remained essentially the same. What changes were made resulted simply from the rising costs of business. Over time, new officers were added: *sindaci*, or *procuratori*, to handle testamentary donations and other important contributions; *ragionieri* to oversee the treasurers; *provveditori* to examine the entire management, and four night watchmen to guard the tabernacle of the Madonna created around 1333 by Giovanni di Balduccio.

In its first year, the *Compagnia* grew quickly, thanks to the cures attributed to the miraculous image, and it soon developed into the most important confraternity in Florence. The combination of the Marian cult with the care for the spiritual welfare of members deceased already, and the promise of the same in future for living members, was a permanent source of revenue, which was firmly enforced by church and state. According to the statutes of 1329, the *capitani* were under legal obligation to issue *lectere d'amonitione* (dunning letters) from the bishop to all notaries in the city and its surroundings to insure that all testamentary legacies and donations of every kind to the *Compagnia* should be delivered within half a month to the treasurers. In the municipal decrees of 1331, 1339, 1344, and 1347, the rights of the *Compagnia* were protected by the government against debtors in arrears, and in all disputes regarding legacies that had been made during the months of the Black Plague in 1348. The proceedings of the *Compagnia* from 1291 to 1347 show that its annual earnings were high from the very beginning; that from 1291 to 1327, they fluctuated between 3,000 and 5,000 *libre* (pounds). This annual figure doubled from 1328 to 1330; by 1331 it had almost tripled, and it remained for many years at this level. This enabled the confraternity to perform a number of charities. A description of Florence, Von Frey's *Florentie urbis et reipublice descriptio* (1339), mentions that the *Compagnia* in that year distributed 10,000 *libre* to the poor.

By the end of 1348 the *Compagnia* had accumulated so much money and property that the Florentine government intervened, decreeing on November 13 of that year that the brotherhood must sell its real estate to the city. This was possibly brought on by irregularities in the management of the confraternity's business. On July 20, 1349, the government decreed a change in the manner by which the *capitani* were chosen, which resulted in a radical restructuring of the organization: its members were deprived of the right to nominate *capitani*. Instead, the government was to choose between two candidates from each quarter of the city. In effect, the *capitani* became municipal officers and the *Compagnia* ceased to be a private and independent institution. It was barred by the municipality from political activity, and gradually went into decline.

The change in the structure of the confraternity's administration, which did not affect its religious and social functions, must have been exercised to commission the elegant tabernacle that Orcagna began in 1352. In 1349, however, Giovanni di Balduccio's shrine still existed. Two factors may have led to the commissioning of the new tabernacle between 1349 and 1352: first, the confraternity's inordinate wealth, and secondly, the desire of the city government to assert its authority by taking charge of the expenditure of the confraternity's funds.

THE ARTIST ORCAGNA

Andreas Cionis vocatus Orcagna: thus was the artist enrolled in 1344 in the registry of painters in the *Arte dei Medici e Speziali*, the guild of the doctors and pharmacists, to which painters also belonged. The nickname Orcagna was derived from *archagnolo* (archangel). The contemporaries who called him that must have based it on his character and efficiency. Orcagna was distinguished as a painter and, later, as an architect and sculptor; previous to this he is said to have been a poet. In short, he was an early example of the "universal man" of Renaissance Florence.

The date of Orcagna's birth is not known; it was probably somewhere between 1315 and 1320. Nor is it known with whom the artist studied his craft; his apprenticeship would have begun in 1329, at the earliest, and ended somewhere around 1337/39 at the latest. His brothers Nardo and Jacopo were also painters; another brother, Matteo, was a sculptor. Nardo, evidently slightly younger, died before May 16, 1366. Matteo lived until 1389/90; and Jacopo, until 1398.

Orcagna is first documented on January 19, 1343 after he had failed to complete a certain task for the *Compagnia di Gesù Pellegrino* at Santa Maria Novella; there was a complaint that he had made many errors and would not follow orders. Apparently, it was not a case of poor craftsmanship, but a dispute over artistic interpretation. A young artist who defended his work even against an important patron was certainly strong-minded.

Orcagna's earliest surviving works are a frescoed tondo in the entrance hall of the municipal prison representing the expulsion of the Duke of Athens from Florence, probably painted soon after that event; and a monumental fresco in Santa Croce depicting the *Triumph of Death*, the *Last Judgement*, and *Hell*, which was probably painted around 1344/45 on the wall of the right aisle; only two large fragments are left. Orcagna may have executed this first large commission with the assistance of a workshop, a prerequisite for matriculation in the Florentine guild. Both the prison tondo and the Santa Croce fresco are clearly innovative work. Here the young Orcagna, as his sculptural treatment of figures and emphatic compositions attest, was influenced by Maso di Banco's frescoes in the St. Sylvester Chapel of the Bardi di Vernio family in Santa Croce; his realization of pictorial space, and his framing with illusionistic architecture also shows the influence of Taddeo Gaddi's frescoes in the Baroncelli chapel in the same church.

A panel painting of the *Annunciation* signed by Orcagna and dated 1346, now in a private collection in Milan, was unfortunately heavily restored during the past fifty years, as old photographs attest. During this disastrous restoration, the shape of the upper part of the picture was severely altered. Originally intended as an altarpiece for the church of San Remigio in Florence, this *Annunciation* was an independent work, much in the tradition of the great altarpieces of the Sienese painters Simone Martini and Ambrogio Lorenzetti.

Orcagna's next creation, a triptych dated 1350 (now in the Rijksmuseum, Amsterdam) that was ordered for the altar of the Ansanus chapel of Santa Maria Maggiore in Florence, bears the inscription of Tommaso Baronci. The altar was against the wall of the left aisle next to the chancel, which the donor had also caused to be decorated with a fresco, now lost, but of which two photographs exist. Located above a socle of imitation marble, this fresco depicted two scenes, one above the other, from the life of St. Thomas, the donor's patron saint. Careful study of the existing photographs of this fresco indicates that it was painted by a coworker from Orcagna's workshop. The triptych, however, may well be by Orcagna himself. The manner of the enthroned Madonna with the Christ Child, between Saints Mary Magdalene and Ansanus, suggests that she is in another sphere than that of the saints, although there is no break in the pictorial space of the three panels; such a break can be observed in Simone Martini's *Annunciation Triptych* of 1333. In the Baronci triptych, the central figure seems weightless, in sharp contrast to the heavy figures of the standing saints. This manner of portraying the central figure also appears in the Strozzi altarpiece in the church of Santa Maria Novella (signed and dated 1357), which had been commissioned in 1354, but the proportions differ. The figures in the earlier, Rijksmuseum triptych are considerably more compact than those in the Strozzi altarpiece, but they are similar in this respect to the frescoes of the *Triumph of Death*, the *Last Judgement*, and *Hell*.

These paintings all bear witness to Orcagna's artistic development. They represent his early style and his development upon completion of the now lost frescoes of the choir chapel of Santa Maria Novella, which were presumably close in style to his best known work, the Strozzi altarpiece. (Orcagna's frescoes in the choir chapel, the colossal walls of which measure 12 or 13 x 24.5 meters, were replaced by those of Domenico Ghirlandaio during 1486/89.) In the Santa Maria Novella choir were scenes from the life of the Virgin on the left side, and from the life of John the Baptist on the right. This remarkable iconographic program, probably devised by the great Dominican preacher Fra Jacopo Passavanti, expounds the parallel lives of Mary and John the Baptist, both of whom were precursors of Christ and incarnations of *humilitas*, which the Dominicans, since the time of Thomas Aquinas, considered the first step on the pathway to God.

Unfortunately, only the thirty-four figures in the quatrefoils of the vault decoration remain of Orcagna's paintings; these were executed between 1348/49 and 1352/53. With this gigantic work, Orcagna must have been led to conceive of figures which presumably led to the large-scale conceptions found in the Strozzi altarpiece.

The Dominicans commissioned the decoration of the choir chapel of their church in 1348, at the height of the devastation of the Black Plague, which killed half of the population of Florence between the spring and fall of that year. Later that same year there was a search for a master painter to work on a polyptych for the church of San Giovanni

Fuorcivitas in Pistoia; in one of the church's record books, possibly written in 1349, six of the best painters in Florence were listed in connection with the painting; below Taddeo Gaddi, who received the commission, appear the names of Orcagna and his brother, Nardo di Cione, who was at that time a partner in his brother's workshop.

From 1352, Orcagna was registered in the *Arte dei Maestri di Pietre e Legnami*, the guild of stone masons and carpenters, probably because he had to direct a workshop in the guild's area of expertise as he started his work on the tabernacle for Orsanmichele. In addition to this major project, in 1354 Orcagna concluded an agreement with Tommaso di Rosello Strozzi to create a polyptych for the family chapel in Santa Maria Novella. The contract stipulated the dimensions of the work, set a time limit for completion at twenty months, required good quality pigments to be used (gold and silver are expressly mentioned), and specified the number of figures. Orcagna was to be paid the splendid fee of 200 gold florins for this work. At the same time, his brother Nardo was to paint frescoes on the walls of the Chapel: the *Last Judgement* on the wall behind the altar, *Paradise* on the left wall, and *Hell* on the right.

The frescoes and the polyptych are part of a program devised by the Dominican scholar, Pietro di Ubertino Strozzi. The altarpiece, as the focal element in the chapel, emerges from the background of the *Last Judgement, Paradise* and *Hell*. Christ appears in the middle of the polyptych like a vision, throned in the heavenly light of a cherubim-bordered mandorla in the space between St. Thomas Aquinas and St. Peter, behind whom are Mary and John the Baptist. Next are St. Michael and St. Catherine on the left side and St. Paul and

The Strozzi altarpiece, painted by Orcagna between 1354 and 1357 for the Strozzi family chapel in Santa Maria Novella, Florence.

33

St. Lawrence on the right. Christ holds out a book to Thomas Aquinas and two keys to Peter. This *traditio legis et clavium* is an iconographic type traceable to the fifth century. What is remarkable about this portrayal is that St. Paul has been forced from his accustomed place of prominence, suggesting that Christ has entrusted Church doctrine to St. Thomas Aquinas and to the Dominicans, while the Church's authority is entrusted to St. Peter, and through him, to the pope. Thus, the Strozzi altarpiece shows Thomas and Peter, representing the Church, placed in front of Mary and John, who together with Christ form a deesis, connecting the theme of divine intercession with that of the Last Judgement. The intercessors, Mary and John, are shown together with representatives of the Church; thus, the Strozzi altarpiece teaches, the church itself offers divine intercession. The saints portrayed are also patrons of the donor's family: St. Thomas represents the donor himself, St. Catherine his wife, St. Peter the author of the program, and St. Paul a member of the family named in the commission contract as the "appraiser" of the work.

The Strozzi altarpiece has been completely misunderstood until recently, as a work without pictorial space, dominated by the flatness of its surface. But the vision of Christ, which breaks into the scene and eliminates space, presupposes the presence of space in the picture. The polyptych, an illusionistic canopy, covers an area defined by punch-worked spiral columns tooled into the gold background, and by two actual spiral columns in the foreground of the frame; in front, additional spiral columns are suggested by empty pedestals and hanging capitals. The painting's spatial depth corresponds to the red-carpeted floor in the area between the arched frame and the punch-worked spiral columns on the gold background. The rather voluminous figures are each carefully set against another. Here Orcagna has achieved a remarkable fusion of the spatial and the physical with the overriding planimetric design of a large triangle.

The work on the tabernacle in Orsanmichele, begun in 1352, was far from finished when Orcagna completed the Strozzi altarpiece in 1357. He then turned to yet another architecturally challenging task: the construction of the Gothic cathedral of Florence. Between 1357 and 1367, Orcagna was occupied with, among other things, problems in the architect's plan; he was also an active participant in the many discussions concerning this project, and in 1358 he had even made a model of the pillars. All this distracted Orcagna from painting and claimed much of his time. When the completion date for the work on the tabernacle approached, he took on another project. On June 14, 1358, he agreed with the cathedral authorities in Orvieto to accept the position of director of the building site in fourteen months' time, after the Orsanmichele tabernacle was finished. He was certainly chosen for this project because of his experience in coordinating masonry, paintings, mosaics, and sculpture. However, after some preparatory visits to Orvieto, Orcagna was active there for only nine months, from October 18, 1359 until March 11, 1360, and from August/September until December 1360. During this time he finished a mosaic of the *Baptism of Christ* on the gable over the left portal of the main façade.

Probably at the beginning of 1360, Orcagna and his workshop decorated the front wall of the refectory of Santo Spirito in Florence—or at least a part of it—with a fresco of the *Last Supper* and the *Crucifixion*, one over the other. Around 1365 he may have created a triptych for the high altar of Santi Apostoli, now in the Museo dell' Accademia, Florence. In this depiction of Pentecost, the artist again demonstrated his mastery of composition, integrating physical and spatial description with a pattern-like treatment of the picture-plane. Here we can also see a change in the chromatic tone of his palette; his more subdued colors suggest the influence of frescoes executed by Giovanni da Milano in the Rinuccini Chapel at Santa Croce.

The last of Orcagna's surviving works is probably his panel of the *Madonna of Humility* now in the National Gallery of Art, Washington, which depicts the Madonna sitting on the floor holding the child Jesus, to whom God the Father is sending down the dove of the Holy Ghost. This portrayal of the Trinity had its example in the relief of the Madonna created by Tino di Camaino for the tomb of St. Raynerius in Pisa's cathedral. While it draws the spectator's eyes to the human nature of Christ in a moving, sympathetic way, the appearance of God the Father and the Holy Spirit certify the divine nature of the child and, at the same time, Mary's special sanctity as God's mother and intercessor.

Orcagna had been working a year on the plans for the cathedral choir, when he entered into an agreement on September 15, 1367 with the powerful *Arte del Cambio* (the guild of money changers) to paint a triptych with the evangelist Matthew in its central panel for one of the pilasters in Orsanmichele. He undertook this commission even though he was obviously behind in his other work. Somewhat later, on November 24, the *Compagnia della Madonna di Orsanmichele* pressured him to complete a painting of the Madonna by the end of December; if he did not, the confraternity threatened, he would be declared a debtor. Orcagna was not able to comply with this warning and was taken to task on March 13, 1368. He was forced to give up his clothes—predominantly outer clothing—as security. These were returned to him on June 9, after he completed the picture. Although it is tempting to identify this Madonna as the panel in the National Gallery of Art in Washington, such an association is hypothetical.

On August 25, 1368, Orcagna was too ill to work, and the commission of the St. Matthew altar was given to his brother, Jacopo di Cione. The triptych is Jacopo's in design and execution; he seems also to have taken over Orcagna's workshop, since he subsequently was registered with the painters' guild.

Orcagna's illness, which became more severe after the commission was withdrawn, may have brought about his death; the exact date of his demise is unknown. In 1377, however, a notary's document mentions his widow, Francisca, and his daughters, Tessa and Romola, as survivors.

III
ORCAGNA'S TABERNACLE AS ARCHITECTURE

When Orcagna created the tabernacle for the miraculous Madonna of Orsanmichele during the years 1352 to 1360, he expected that it would be visible in daylight, for at that time the market hall was open on all sides. The light was diminished considerably when the exterior arcades were filled in shortly after Orcagna completed his work, thus preventing it from being seen properly. But for about a quarter of a century now, the tabernacle has been visible by electric light, which illuminates it directly with such intensity that the lustrous colors of its decoration are bleached out. Today one can see something of its original appearance only on its back side, when the door of the oratory is opened by tourists. Then the reflected sunlight shines on its richly painted ornamentation and stained glass mosaics, causing its variegated surfaces to cast multiple shadows.

The abundance of colored and sculptured ornamentation gives the tabernacle the complex character of goldsmith's work. An example of such work that Orcagna probably knew is the 97-centimeter-high reliquary of St. Savinus, created in the 1340s by Ugolino di Vieri and Viva di Lando, now in Orvieto's cathedral museum. The structure of this piece corresponds closely to that of Orcagna's tabernacle: a polygonal plinth supported by lions, which carries a socle on which rests the tabernacle itself. Inside is a statuette of the Madonna under a dome, which is supported by a drum. A platform above the tabernacle's ogival arcade supports a tower and cupola, which is crowned with a statuette of an angel. No other baldachin is as close to Orcagna's tabernacle canopy in structure and arrangement as that of the reliquary of St. Savinus. It quite possibly suggested the extraordinary and innovative element of the drum, which Orcagna used to support his cupola.

Orcagna's tabernacle is raised in several stages above the floor of the grain market hall. The first level extends on all sides to the adjacent bays of the building, its broad surface inlaid with ornamental marble pieces, so that the shrine appears to be surrounded by a carpet. The next two levels are ornamented in great detail, and have polygonal ground plans, which reflect that of the tabernacle itself. A marble balustrade stands at the edge of the upper level, its square frames filled with bronze grill work. At each of its four corners is a pilaster, on which lions guard the foot of a spiral colonnette, at the top of which stands a statuette of an angel. These exterior features are well known; the tabernacle's interior, however, has remained almost completely unknown until now.

The tabernacle itself rises over a square ground plan. The corner piers rest on pronounced bases; the arches between the piers are closed by low walls which form a socle. At the height of the arches, a groined vault covers the tabernacle and creates a platform. The wall in the blind arch at the rear houses a very narrow but passable staircase, which runs from the ground floor up to the platform; because of this staircase the wall is very thick, and intrudes into the interior space of the shrine, where it holds Daddi's panel of the Madonna. The exterior side is decorated by a monumental relief.

On the platform above the tabernacle's vaulting, the corner piers continue as pinnacles; free-standing gables rise above the arches, and the area in between is occupied by a high, octagonal drum with eight round arches, which tower above the ogival cupola that is still visible over the gables. Statues of angels stand on the points of the gables, and a statue of St. Michael crowns the apex of the cupola, which rises almost to the keystone of the market hall's vault.

The entrance to the tabernacle's interior is distinctly awkward, which is undoubtedly the reason that it has remained almost unknown. To begin with, the marble balustrade prevents the visitor from directly entering the tabernacle. The bronze gate is on the north side of the balustrade, while the door to the shrine is on the east (rear) side of the socle. The door opening is only 99 centimeters high and 58.5 centimeters (= 1 braccia) wide. It is closed by an inlaid wooden door; behind it, at the same height as the door, is a small corridor, 110 centimeters long. The space is so small that one can only walk to the interior on one's knees. It has been wrongly suggested that the tabernacle is a miniature "church" for the miracle-working image of Mary, to be entered only by a select group of people, certain members of the confraternity from the more important Florentine families, perhaps. Orcagna's tabernacle is certainly not intended for people to enter, except for officials of the *Compagnia* or musicians, invisible from the outside. It was built exclusively as a shrine for the miraculous image, as a closer examination of the interior bears out.

Recent study of the interior of the tabernacle has shown that the three arches could be opened or closed by raising or lowering a set of shutters, which slide along tracks. These tracks can be blocked by movable parts of the moulding in the front corners of the tabernacle. When this is done, the screens are locked into position. To open the arches, the mouldings in the corner piers must be pushed in so that the shutters can be brought down on the inner side of the socle to small spaces under ground. Long, narrow marble slabs with two iron rings on their exterior sides lie along the floor beside the socle. Using the rings, the slabs can be pushed into the socle walls. With the slabs in this position, the shutters in the arcade openings could be lowered into slots in the floor. With the interior side of the socle wall being 1.5 meters high, and the opening of the arcades 3.9 meters high, the slot for the lowered shutters must have a depth of 2.4 meters. Each guide track has a small, square opening onto the platform of the cupola at the apex of the arch. Apparently, the shutters were lowered by a pole or cord from this platform. The narrow stairway in the partition wall of the rear arch was thus constructed for the use of the shutter operators.

The architecture of Orcagna's tabernacle was modeled upon Giovanni di Balduccio's shrine of 1333, as the illustration and description in the confraternity's *Capitoli* confirm; in accordance with its predecessor, Orcagna's tabernacle was built upon a quadratic ground plan, enclosed on all sides in a socle area, and accessible only through a small gate in the rear. It has three open arches, and the wall of its blind rear arch bears the miraculous image. However, some special features of Orcagna's structure indicate that in the interim the confraternity revised its requirements. Orcagna's balustrade prevented visitors from directly approaching the tabernacle. For that reason, there is no provision for alms boxes on the balustrade. Unlike those of its predecessor,

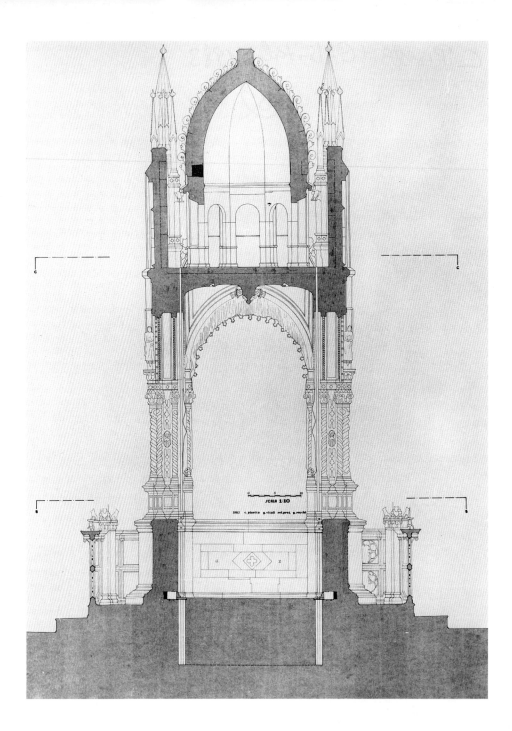

Section drawing of Orcagna's tabernacle.

the arches of Orcagna's shrine could be closed by heavy wooden shutters. Thus, apparently, two clerks were not required to guard it day and night.

Orcagna's tabernacle was covered by a groined vault, and above that, by a cupola raised on a platform over the vaulting. This is decidedly not the sort of architecture where one would expect to see a cupola, nor is there any technical reason to have one. In fact, it makes sense not to raise the tabernacle space too high, for only small sections of the canopy are visible. The confraternity and Orcagna must therefore have had a special reason to furnish the new tabernacle, unlike the previous one, with a cupola.

There is a meaningful association between the cupola design and the cult of the Virgin, since cupola architecture is specifically associated with sanctuaries of the Madonna. The cathedrals in Pisa, Siena, and Florence, all of them domed, are dedicated to Mary; according to a plan of around 1370, the Cappella di Piazza in Siena was also to have a dome. Similarly, of the niches on Orsanmichele's exterior piers, which are provided to house images of the patron saints of the guilds, the only one executed in a cupola form is the one for the doctors and pharmacists (*Arte dei Medici e Speziali*), which contains a statue of the enthroned Madonna, the guild's patroness. Thus, the cupola of Orcagna's tabernacle refers specifically to Mary; its enclosed housing may also have been understood as an architectural symbol for Mary's virginity.

But the reason for designing a tabernacle with a cupola may have been more than iconographic. The cupola signified the greater prestige of the confraternity, and demonstrated the virtuosity of its builder. Likewise, through his tabernacle, Orcagna the painter became Orcagna the architect; its design established his reputation as versatile artist of extraordinary vision and ability. Although his tabernacle is a monumentalized reliquary—in effect goldsmith's work as architecture—the idea of erecting a cupola on a platform had never been contemplated on this scale before. With his use of a drum to support it, Orcagna gave this structural element from the reliquary of St. Savinus new life as an architectural form.

A matter still in dispute is the possible relationship of Orcagna's tabernacle dome to the chancel cupola of the Cathedral of Florence. Does Orcagna's structure owe its conception to Arnolfo di Cambio's hypothetical first cathedral project (ca. 1295), which—as many believe—included in its plan a chancel with a cupola? Or did it serve as a model for the cathedral plan sometime prior to June 19, 1357, when that project is first documented, or for the plan of 1366/67, which gave the chancel its shape? Unfortunately, nothing has come to light which can answer these questions. It is simply not known what the Arnolfian project looked like.

Even if Arnolfo di Cambio already had projected a chancel dome, which is questionable, Orcagna's tabernacle cupola could hardly be traced to it. Rather, it reflects the miniature architecture of the reliquary of St. Savinus.

Regarding the Cathedral planning of the middle 1350s and of 1366/67, Orcagna's tabernacle is of interest. The artist is first mentioned in the cathedral records of June 19, 1357, regarding the determination of the measurements and structure of the nave, as well as the measurements of a base for a cupola. Orcagna was present on July 5, 1357 when the cornerstone of the first pier was consecrated. From June until August 1357, there was a competition between Orcagna and the cathedral architect Francesco Talenti over the form of the nave pillars; Talenti's model emerged the winner.

When, in 1364, design problems still remained unsolved, Orcagna participated in a discussion of the forms of the windows in the clerestory and the position of the gallery in the nave. Later, in discussions concerning the design of the chancel dome (1366/67), Orcagna was from the very beginning one of the leading masters of the committee of the stone masons and painters, which brought about the project's success. Given his experience as architect of the Orsanmichele tabernacle cupola, the artist was almost certainly the central figure in the evolution of the idea of a drum under the Cathedral chancel dome.

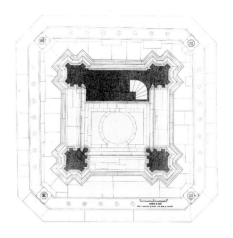

Floor plan of Orcagna's tabernacle.

IV
FORM AND MEANING

Orcagna's tabernacle was created as a monstrance for a miraculous painting of the Virgin through which her beneficial power manifested itself in this world, and gave evidence of her effectiveness as a merciful intercessor in the life of the world to come. In creating this extraordinary shrine, Orcagna intended that every detail would have symbolic significance. Emblematic meaning is as evident in the architecture as it is in the decorative elements.

THE ARCHITECTURE

Numerous literary sources associate enclosed structures (towers, tabernacles, cities, castles) with the Virgin. But although enclosed, Giovanni di Balduccio's tabernacle could not be thought of in this symbolic sense, for, according to the *Capitoli della Compagnia della Madonna di Orsanmichele*, the confraternity had to have clerks stationed by it day and night in order to receive offerings. For Orcagna's shrine they made no such provision. His tabernacle is not only enclosed, it is completely encircled by a marble barrier, whose spiral corner pillars each bear an angel holding a candelabrum. This enclosure may well have been understood, like the tradional *hortus conclusus* (the enclosed garden), as a symbol of virginity. In any case the tabernacle itself, which is surrounded by the walls (roughly 1.5 meters) of the socle area, and whose arches could be shut off by retractable wooden shutters, is unmistakably the architectural symbol of Mary's virginity.

Cupolas have traditionally symbolized the cosmos, the celestial dome that vaults the earth. Moreover, as we have seen, a cupola appears to have been the preferred construction for churches dedicated to the Virgin as the intercessor for all mankind. This idea has its origins in the early Christian era. In 610, for example, the Pantheon in Rome was consecrated as *Santa Maria Rotunda*. Thus, Orcagna's tabernacle cupola seems to have been intended as another symbol of Mary.

THE DECORATION

The decoration of Orcagna's tabernacle is uniquely rich and varied, and its motifs are extraordinary. Nevertheless, these have been virtually ignored up until now. This is particularly remarkable, since literary sources testify that medieval thought was inexhaustible in devising symbols. All manner of plants, animals, minerals, implements, and natural phenomena could be assigned meanings. It is impossible that the ornamental motifs on the tabernacle were conceived merely as decoration. Their abundance alone suggests that they must have meant something.

Noteworthy as a decorative motif, first of all, are the seashells, which densely border the reliefs in the socle area. Symmetrically arranged, they line the arches and the imposts of the pillars. A shell framed by a six-sided star occupies the center of every section of the vault. These

vault. These shells and stars as well as the snails on the friezes in the arches, reveal an immediate connection to the Virgin. The seashell was a particular and universally understood symbol for the Virgin birth, for the shell was considered the mother of the light-begotten pearl, which symbolized Christ. The snail also stood for the virginity of Mary, due to the popular belief that the creature came into being from mud, without procreation.

The rose is still another emblem of the Virgin in the tabernacle decoration. But is the floral ornament on the marble barrier surrounding the tabernacle a rose? Are the blossoming buds between the crockets on the groin of the cupola to be understood as roses? This is not clear. The flowers on the capitals of the spiral colonnettes flanking the arches, however, are indisputably roses. The rose, loaded with different meanings, such as chastity and charity, was a favorite symbol for the Virgin Mary; its presence on the capitals, however, may have had no specific meaning.

For his tabernacle, Orcagna created figurative reliefs, statues, and decorative sculptures of varying sizes. Surprisingly, however, the gables over the arches were not provided with a relief of Christ, as in the earlier tabernacle of 1333, but with only a decorative star composed of two equal, intersecting triangles. In such a prominent position, a single star cannot have been merely ornamental; a symbolic meaning must have been intended. Possibly, it is the star of Heaven, which, through its purity and clarity, shines as brightly as all the saints; or, it may represent the *Stella Maris* from the Litany of the Virgin, the star of the sea, which guides mankind, like mariners to a safe harbor, to paradise.

These themes—virginity, the rose of charity, and the star of the sea—speak of redemption. They are communicated, in perfect accord with the architectural symbolism, through the language of ornament.

THE SCULPTURE

The marble barrier, which encloses the Marian tabernacle as a symbol of Mary's virginity, presents its compact corner piers as bases for the lion-guarded spiral colonnettes. The lions may symbolize the Florentine Commune, with its associations of freedom and patriotism. On each of the four colonnettes stands a candle-bearing angel, to provide light when the shrine was open and the miraculous image of the Madonna was on view.

The socle is the base on which the tabernacle stands. Likewise, the reliefs on the socle form the foundation for the sculptural program. There is not just one relief cycle, but three, each one a self-sufficient whole; taken together, however, they amplify each other's meaning.

The first cycle presents the Life of Mary in ten scenes, which literally lead the spectator to the miraculous image. The cycle begins on the left (north) side of the tabernacle, continues to the front (west) and right (south) sides, then around to the back (east). There are two reliefs from the Life of Mary on each of the four walls of the socle; the last two scenes occupy the wall filling the rear arch, the front of which bears the miraculous image.

The second cycle is an unusually extensive series of the Virtues. One relief of each of the three Theological Virtues, Faith, Hope, and Charity, sits between two scenes of the Life of Mary on each socle wall, except for the rear wall, where the center is occupied by the small door leading into the interior of the tabernacle. Thus the allegories of the Virtues and the scenes of Mary's life form an alternating sequence.

Overleaf: Angels from the stone frame of Bernardo Daddi's miraculous Madonna.

Set at the corners of the four piers are reliefs of the four Cardinal Virtues: Prudence, Justice, Fortitude, and Temperance. In addition, there are depictions of related Virtues on either side of each Cardinal Virtue, on the adjacent sides of the piers.

The third cycle includes eight reliefs of prophets and patriarchs, as well as Tobias and Luke, which are set on the sides of the corner piers that border the walls of the socle. Each figure is thus next to a scene from the Life of Mary. Another relief of a prophet, which must be considered part of this cycle, is set in the wall immediately under the monumental relief containing the two final scenes from the Life of Mary on the wall of the rear arch. Each relief is arranged with the greatest deliberation in its appointed place on the tabernacle, and thus within the context of the program.

The cycle of Mary's life contains the following scenes: the *Birth of the Virgin* and the *Presentation of the Virgin in the Temple* (left); the *Marriage of the Virgin* and the *Annunciation* (front); the *Nativity of Christ* and the *Adoration of the Magi* (right); and finally the *Presentation of Christ in the Temple* and the *Annunciation of the Death of the Virgin* (rear). It ends with a relief, on the wall of the rear arch, of the *Death and Assumption of the Virgin*, on the side opposite the miraculous image.

The textual sources for the reliefs of the Marian cycle are the *Gospel According to St. James*, which relates the history of the Virgin up to the Nativity; the apocryphal *Gospel According to St. Matthew*; the *Gospel of the Birth of Mary*; and the *Golden Legend* of Jacopo da Voragine, from the end of the thirteenth century, which was probably the most important text to Orcagna. Visual sources for the cycle may have been Giotto's frescoes in the Scrovegni chapel in Padua (1305/09), as well as the now destroyed frescoes dedicated to the Assumption of Mary that Giotto painted in the choir of Santa Croce in Florence; other examples may have been various individual depictions by Pietro and Ambrogio Lorenzetti from 1320 to 1350, or Taddeo Gaddi's fresco cycle in the Baroncelli chapel in Santa Croce (1330/33).

As regards artistic and iconographic intentions, this last cycle probably influenced Orcagna the most. The plan of this chapel was similar to that of the tabernacle; it included a cycle of the virtues in the tondi of the vault and window jambs, and a cycle of figures from the Old Testament in quatrefoils on the transverse arch of the Marian cycle.

Unlike those of Taddeo Gaddi in the Baroncelli chapel, the virtues on Orcagna's tabernacle are not placed alongside a Marian cycle without meaning. On the contrary, they are interwoven with the scenes of Mary's life so that the Marian cycle and that of the virtues form a many-sided and deeply significant unity.

Among the many virtues, there are seven principal ones: the three Theological Virtues—Faith, Hope, and Charity—and the four Cardinal Virtues—Prudence, Justice, Fortitude, and Temperance. The four Cardinal Virtues, which were dependent on correct action, were originally analyzed by Plato and Aristotle (cf. Plato, *Rep.* IV 427ff.; Aristotle, *Nic. Eth.* IV 3,6). Cicero and Macrobius increased the number of the virtues through a system of classification, which greatly influenced the composition of cycles of the Virtues in Gothic art (Cicero, *De offic.* I 5, *De inv.* II 53ff., *De fin.* II 21; Macrobius, *In somn. Scip.* I 8). The three Theological Virtues were based on the teachings of St. Paul (I *Cor.* 13), and are therefore specifically Christian.

On the tabernacle, each of the three Theological Virtues is set between two scenes of Mary's life, thereby implying that these virtues constitute the center of her moral existence. Thus, the three reliefs on any given side of the tabernacle form an intellectual whole. Between the *Birth of the Virgin* and the *Presentation in the Temple* appears Faith as the fundamental force in Mary's life. Faith was manifested also through Mary's mother, St. Anne, because she had believed, contrary to all probability, that her daughter would be conceived. Between the scenes of the *Marriage of the Virgin* and the *Annunciation* is Hope, for salvation and eternal peace. Since they are on the front of the socle, the three scenes function as a predella for the miraculous image of the Madonna holding the Christ Child, bearing testimony to the fact that Mary is divinely blessed, and is a powerful mediator for mankind. Situated between the *Nativity* and the *Adoration of the Magi*, Charity is identified as the reason for both the incarnation of Christ and for Mary's blessed virginity. The figure of Charity, who is nursing a child, echoes Mary's image, thereby implying that Mary is herself an *exemplum* of this virtue.

The Cardinal Virtues occupy the four corners of Orcagna's tabernacle. They are arranged in the order assigned by Aristotle and Cicero, which was continued in Christian teaching: Prudence, Justice, Fortitude, and Temperance. Each of these is accompanied by two subordinate virtues, related to them exactly as found in Thomas Aquinas's *Summa Theologica*. For example, on the northeastern corner pillar, Prudence, which comprises goodness and aids in its acquisition, is flanked by Erudition and Ingenuity. On the northwestern corner pier, Justice, which represents the law, and acknowledges and respects its compliance, is placed with Obedience and Devotion. Fortitude, which combats evil and strengthens mankind in fulfilling its obligations, is on the southwestern pier along with Patience and Perseverance; here Patience stands for strength in holding fast to goodness, and Perseverance for strength in persisting in the exercise of good deeds. Temperance, which disposes humanity to moderation as it corresponds to reason, is on the southeastern corner pier, together with Humility and Virginity, virtues that are specific expressions of Temperance. As the Life of Mary is interspersed with the Virtues, Mary herself is portrayed as the incarnation of righteousness.

In addition to the Virtues, each of the four corner piers also carries two Biblical figures, including prophets, patriarchs, the apocryphal hero Tobias, and St. Luke, each holding a scroll or book bearing inscriptions and names; a ninth prophet appears beneath the relief of the *Death and Assumption of the Virgin*, behind the miraculous image. The inscriptions of Tobias and Luke overlap neighboring scenes of the Life of Mary, and thereby emphasize them. The encroachment of these two figures on those scenes is similar in effect to the gesture of the ninth figure in the cycle, whose right hand, breaking out of his frame, points upward to the *Death and Assumption of the Virgin*.

Orcagna depicted a cycle of angels in the reliefs at the centers of the corner piers: four angels on each of both front piers and three on each of the back piers, which frame the blind arch. With a certain economy of design, Orcagna produced all the angel figures in pairs, except for those on the back piers. One pair carries cornucopiae and bundles of grain, the other cudgels and shields inscribed with a Cross, which is reminiscent of the coat of arms of the Florentine people, the *Croce del Popolo*. The meaning of these emblems is uncertain. In any case, the Virgin is surrounded by a chorus of angels in the miraculous image itself, all of whom are shown kneeling in devotion and reverence. Another set of ten angels, sculpted in full figure in high relief, surround the panel as a frame. On each side of the painting hover five angels, one over the other. Both lower angels play musical instruments, one the violin, the other the zither. The next two (on either side) are singers carrying long-stemmed lilies, symbols of the purity and virginity of Mary. The next two are musicians, playing cymbals. The two above are four-winged seraphim holding palm branches, symbolizing Paradise. The uppermost pair of angels carry the sculpted curtain which is draped around the painting, while the angels carrying the lilies and palm branches pull it aside to reveal the miraculous image to devout spectators. Orcagna placed a third angel choir of cherubim who turn toward the Virgin and Child in the spandrels above the arch. The multitude of angels venerating the Blessed Virgin emphasizes her high rank in heaven.

In another cycle, the Apostles too, are gathered around the miraculous image. Their statues stand on the corner piers at the height of the arches, holding books or scrolls on which are written the articles of the Creed, which, since the fourth century, the Apostles were believed to have written. Unlike the cycles of the Life of Mary and the Virtues, which begin at the northeastern corner pier, the Apostle cycle begins at the right end of the front side; specifically, Peter stands on the side of the southwestern corner pier which borders the front of the tabernacle.

Peter, identified by his key, begins: *Credo in Deum patrem omnipotentem, creatorem caeli et terrae*. Andrew, to his right, adds: *Et in Iesum Christum filium eius unicum, dominum nostrum*. James the Greater continues: *Qui conceptus est de Spiritu Sancto, natus ex Maria virgine*. On the southeastern pillar are John the Divine: *Passus sub Pontio Pilato, crucifixus, mortuus et sepultus*; the beardless, youthful Thomas: *Descendit ad inferos, tertia die resurrexit a mortuis*; and James the Less: *Ascendit ad caelos, sedet ad dexteram Dei patris omnipotentis*. The scroll of the first figure on the northeastern pier, the young, beardless Apostle Philip, is blank; his inscription should read: *Inde venturus est iudicare vivos et mortuos*. He is followed by Bartholomew: *Credo in Spiritum Sanctum*; and Matthew: *Sanctam ecclesiam catholicam, sanctorum communionem*. On the northwestern corner pier the cycle ends with Simon: *Remissionem peccatorum*; Thaddeus: *Carnis resurrectionem*; and Matthias: *Vitam aeternam*. Thus, Orcagna arranged the Apostles so that the miraculous image of the Madonna can be viewed together with the beginning and the end of the cycle of Apostles and the Creed. Quite possibly connections between the articles of the Creed and particular scenes of the Life of Mary were also intended. In any case, the *natus ex Maria virgine* ["born of the Virgin Mary"] of James the Greater corresponds with the relief of the *Nativity*, and the *Ascendit ad caelos* ["he/she ascended to Heaven"] of James the Less corresponds with the *Assumption of the Virgin*, as does Philip's comment on the Last Judgment. Another aspect may be important in understanding the Apostles: they stand on the piers of the tabernacle, a position that portrays them as pillars of the Church. This iconography corresponds to the association of the Apostles with the articles of the Creed. Thus in this cycle, Mary is enthroned as Queen of the Apostles and Mother of the Church.

Above the arcades and directly under the gables and corner pinnacles, a cycle of twenty-eight reliefs surrounds the tabernacle: fourteen angels and fourteen figures with scrolls, books, and other attributes are arranged in alternating sequence. David and Noah are clearly identifiable by their attributes of the harp and the ark, while Abraham and Isaac are portrayed together in one relief. There is also a scroll-bearing king with crown and fur collar, possibly Solomon. Based on the four identifiable subjects—Noah, Abraham with Isaac, Solomon and David—the fourteen reliefs would seem to be depictions of figures from the Old Testament. Their number, fourteen, supports this possibility, for Matthew writes at the beginning of his Gospel regarding the ancestors of Christ (1:17): "So all the generations from Abraham to David are fourteen generations; and from David until the carrying away into Babylon are fourteen generations; and from the carrying away into Babylon unto Christ are fourteen generations." Since the number of Christ's ancestors totals 3 x 14, the number fourteen strongly suggests these figures are the ancestors of Christ and also of Mary, who descended from the house of David.

The five identifiable figures in the fourteen reliefs are indeed among the ancestors of Christ. Although Matthew's genealogical list extends back only to Abraham, and thus does not include Noah, Noah is listed in the Gospel of Luke (3:23–38),which traces Christ's ancestry back through more than seventy-six names to Adam.

Between the figures of the Ancestors of Mary and Christ are angels in tunics and cloaks, deacon's vestments or copes; two wear armor. All wear diadems, and with one exception, all are winged. Some clasp their hands together or cross their arms as a sign of adoration; others carry scrolls. As heaven's messengers, two angels hold staves, and the two in armor carry shields, one of which is marked with a Florentine lily. This angel, in addition, holds a messenger's staff. Two angels, who occupy the corner position of the front side and consequently can be viewed with the Madonna of the miraculous image, are holding lilies, Marian symbols of virginity. Like the angels enframing the throne of the Madonna, the adoring angels on the piers and the chorus of cherubim, so are the angels in the cycle above the arches among the heavenly host, testifying to the heavenly rank of the Blessed Virgin, the powerful and merciful intercessor for mankind.

On each of the four gables of the tabernacle stands an angel wearing armor. In his left hand he carries a shield, in his right hand, a messenger's staff or sword. These angels, too, are paired. Those on the front and rear gables carry messenger's staves, and their shields are inscribed AVE MARIA; those on the left and right gables carry swords, and their shields are inscribed GRATIA PLENA. Gabriel is not among them, for the bearer of angelic salutations at the *Annunciation* has no need of armament to perform his task; nor is Michael, although he is often depicted in armor and holding a sword, for the figure of this archangel stands on the cupola, surrounded by these four. These angels are guardians, each one facing a different direction, to present the greeting of Gabriel to the Virgin: AVE MARIA—GRATIA PLENA.

Presiding over the four angels on the gables of the tabernacle is the figure of the archangel Michael on the crown of the cupola. Michael stands upright, holding an upraised sword in his right hand. In this context, with the other angels below him, he too may be regarded as a guard. His elevated position marks him as the master of the house, the patron saint of Orsanmichele. Michael's head extends so high that it touches the keystone of the vault of the market hall, in such a way that this stone, with its carved Florentine lily seems like an enormous halo. Thus the statue of Michael establishes a link between the Marian shrine and the building of Orsanmichele, as well as with the city of Florence.

V
THE SCULPTURE AS ART

THE MASTER AND HIS WORKSHOP

Around 1344, Orcagna was registered with the painters of the *Arte dei Medici e Speziali* (the Doctors' and Pharmacists' Guild) because he had to undertake large-scale commissions, for which he had to hire assistants. In 1352 he matriculated in the *Arte dei Maestri di Pietre e Legnami* (Stone Masons' and Carpenters' Guild), since he had received the commission to produce the tabernacle in Orsanmichele, for which he had to set up a second workshop for bricklayers, stone masons, and sculptors.

There may indeed have been a competition for this important project. In late medieval Europe, painters of all ranks competed for such architectural commissions. In 1334, for example, the painter Giotto had presented a proposal for the campanile of the cathedral of Florence, and had begun its execution. During 1366/67, Orcagna himself was among the architects and sculptors who developed the model of the cathedral choir. Although it happened only rarely that painters crossed over into the area of sculpture, it was not totally out of the question. Maso di Banco, to whom the young Orcagna was stylistically deeply indebted, for example, was exceptionally skilled in both arts, according to Lorenzo Ghiberti's *Commentarii*. But Maso, who may have created the tomb for Bishop Tedice Aliotti (ca. 1336) in Santa Maria Novella, as well as two statues for the cathedral campanile, was never a member of the sculptors' guild.

Working relations between painters and sculptors were common; in many cases, the models for sculptures were made by painters. Lorenzo di Bicci, Agnolo Gaddi, and Spinello Aretino, for example, all sketched or painted models for the apostle cycle for the cathedral executed by Piero di Giovanni Tedesco during 1387/90. Often the characteristic manner of the draughtsman is identifiable, even through the stylistic overlay of the sculptor. The reliefs of the Virtues in the Loggia dei Priori (dei Lanzi) in Florence were designed by Agnolo Gaddi and sculpted during 1383/91 by Jacopo di Piero Guidi, Giovanni d'Ambrogio and Giovanni Fetti. Giotto may have designed the reliefs on the campanile of Florence cathedral (1334), and Simone Martini may have designed the statues of an apostle cycle in the cathedral of Siena.

Just what the drawings looked like—none have survived from the mid-fourteenth century—can be surmised only from the depictions of sculptures in paintings. In the fresco cycle in the upper church of San Francesco in Assisi, which—with the participation of various northern, Roman, and Tuscan workshops, including Giotto's—emerged as an important center for the development of Tuscan painting during the last third of the thirteenth century, there are scenes of the legend of St. Francis that correspond to sculptures. In *The Expulsion of the Devil from Arezzo*, for example, the gable of the cathedral choir has painted reliefs; in the *Dirge of the Poor Clares*, there are reliefs and statues on the church façade; and in the *Release of Peter of Alife by the*

Opposite: Detail of Mary and the Christ Child, from the *Nativity* relief on the south socle *(see plates 32–35).*

Intervention of Saint Francis, there are reliefs running around the prison tower in a spiraling frieze, reminiscent of the Roman triumphal column of Trajan. Giotto's grisaille frescoes in the Scrovegni Chapel in Padua (1303/05), particularly the depictions of the virtues and vices, look like a painter's designs for sculpture; each of these personifications is, through modeling in light and shadow, executed three-dimensionally with great vividness, like painted sculpture.

With regard to Orcagna's method of directing his workshop, our only sources of information are the tabernacle and the sculptures themselves. Not only are the carved ornamental and figurative decorations and the marble and glass inlays executed with almost perfect precision, but each marble block from which the tabernacle is built has been worked with exquisite care. Each of the four piers which support the arches, together with their twisted colonnettes, was cut from a single block. The opening and closing of the trap door in the arches' movable marble element, which still functions today, has been cut with the exactness of a precision-instrument maker. Such details of craftsmanship make it clear that from the very beginning, Orcagna employed only first-class stone masons in his workshop. These master craftsmen could not have been trained by Orcagna himself. Whether at any time before 1352 he was involved with others on a sculpture project or worked in marble on his own is not known. Indeed, we do not know if Orcagna actually cut any of the reliefs or figures on the tabernacle himself. It is possible that, stimulated by the example of Maso di Banco, Orcagna attempted, before 1352, to realize some of his figures in marble. At any rate, from 1352 on, he was able, with his workshop, to carry on with an extraordinary precision.

Likewise, we know little of the sculptors in Orcagna's workshop. Stone masons and sculptors underwent the same apprenticeship, the sculptors distinguishing themselves from their fellows as their talent in depicting figures emerged. This talent was always rare, though there were many stone masons available. Even in a city as important as Florence, real sculptors were a scarcity.

Whoever the sculptors that Orcagna hired were, they had a brilliant and energetic master, and they paid close attention to his designs and instructions. Giving evidence to this are the number of figure pairs. Of the four light-bearing angels on the corners of the balustrade that surrounds the tabernacle, those on the right side (front and rear) are based on the same design; the figures strike the same pose, especially where the arms are concerned; the drapery is almost identical, with the belt at the waist and under the breast, and the sleeves bunched, wide above and narrow below; the draping of the stola and the hair style, with eight long locks that hang down the back, are also identical. The two angels on the left side also form a pair; their postures and draperies are fundamentally alike, with the stola as the only deviation. The angels on the gables over the arcades are also paired, bearing shields inscribed AVE MARIA or GRATIA PLENA. In the row of angels enframing the miraculous image, only the angels of the lower pair with violin and zither differ from each other. The angels of the next four pairs were created from the same design but reversed sideways: the next pair, of lily-bearing singers, is followed by a pair of cymbal players, and a pair of seraphim carrying palm branches; the uppermost pair hold the curtain of the miraculous image. The fourteen reliefs with half-figures of angels (seven pairs) located at the centers of the arcade piers are in identical postures of adoration; they carry cornucopiae and bundles of grain, or cudgels and shields. Only one design was necessary for the ring of eight cherubim in the spandrels over the arcade arches. The similarity between the two figures of each pair is remarkable, for they are plainly the work of different masters who adhered strictly to a common pattern. In consequence, we must assume for all the other figures that the sculptors have also followed Orcagna's design.

WORK GROUPS AND SCULPTORS

The photographs published here present the sculptures on the socle and rear wall in proper context; no less than four different sculptors were involved in their realization. Each piece is presumed to be an accurate execution of a design made by Orcagna. The only variation apparent in the sculptures is in the degree of plasticity or rigidity, particularly in the faces.

ORCAGNA

Orcagna was probably an active participant as a sculptor in the tabernacle project. During part of this period, he was also creating the altarpiece for the Strozzi Chapel at Santa Maria Novella. The Virtue *Fides* (Faith) and the *Annunciation of the Death of the Virgin* on the socle, and the *Death and Assumption of the Virgin*, sculpturally correspond to Orcagna's painted depictions in the Strozzi altarpiece. The similarity in figurative conception, in the drapery style, and in the articulation of the faces and hands, is obvious. Both the pose and the drapery of the enthroned *Fides* resemble those of Christ in the altarpiece, her face that of St. Michael in the same work. Both faces are modeled with extraordinary subtlety, their expressions enlivened by the detail with which the iris and pupil are delineated. The refinement of the face of *Fides* communicates a feeling of inspiration from within, such as we see again in the face of Mary, who accepts the news of her approaching death with an expression of beatific joy.

A feeling of heavenly rest can be seen on the countenance of the dead Mary in the *Death of the Virgin*. The demeanors and gestures of the apostles who stand around her bier express varying degrees of sorrow. Only the man in the kerchief at the extreme right in the second row of the relief appears to be a slightly more aloof observer. His face, which is stylistically consistent with the rest of the relief, seems to be a portrait. Vasari believed that this head was indeed Orcagna's self-portrait, which is entirely credible. On the other hand, the face resembles, in its sensitive modeling, that of Thomas Aquinas in the Strozzi altarpiece, which is said to have been a portrait of the donor, Tommaso di Rosello Strozzi. Owing to its relatively large size, the sculptured head seems out of context; moreover, there is a slight unevenness in the smooth background surrounding it. Perhaps Orcagna cut this head somewhat later than the others in the relief.

The figure of Mary in the mandorla of the *Assumption* relief is, in the conception of the figure and in the drapery style, related to the Christ in the Strozzi altarpiece; her face likewise resembles that of the Mary in the same work.

The distinct plasticity, the full volumes, and the extraordinarily sensitive modeling that distinguish these figures, as well as the forceful expressiveness of their faces, make this group peerless in Florentine sculpture during the third quarter of the fourteenth century. But, the sculptures are not stylistically isolated in their place and time; rather, they are the three-dimensional counterparts of Orcagna's painting.

Orcagna was certainly not a student of the sculptor Andrea Pisano, as Vasari claimed. On the contrary, he had the ability to recreate his own style as a sculptor, because he was able to transfer an imagined figure perfectly from the medium of painting to that of sculpture. However, the painter may have assimilated his manner of modelling flesh from the older sculptor's works in Florence and Pisa. With regard to the treatment of flesh, Orcagna may also have studied Nicola Pisano's pulpit reliefs in the cathedral of Siena, for certain resemblances can be seen between the pulpit figures and the forms of Orcagna's tabernacle.

MATTEO DI CIONE (?)

The thirty-one reliefs on the socle were certainly the first sculptures created for the tabernacle. It is remarkable that Orcagna evidently preferred one sculptor, who executed no less than 18 reliefs: the Virtue *Solertia* (Ingenuity) and the neighboring prophet on the northeastern corner pier; the Virtues *Oboedientia*, *Justitia*, and *Devotio*, as well as Luke, on the northwestern corner pier; *Spes* in the center of the socle front and the *Annunciation* relief next to it; on the southwestern corner pier, a prophet, *Patientia*, *Fortitudo*, and a patriarch; *Caritas* in the middle of the south side; a prophet, *Temperantia*, and *Virginitas* on the southeastern corner pier; the depiction of *The Presentation of Christ in the Temple* on the rear side; and, finally, the prophet on the northeastern corner pier.

All the figures of these reliefs designed by Orcagna are characterized by a soft cutting technique. Typical also are the smooth modeling of the hair and the articulation of the features, particularly the eyes and mouth. The forms are not sharply outlined, but rather their edges are gently graduated. Also characteristic are the long, slim, agile fingers.

The sculptor chosen for this work would probably have been commissioned for other projects in Florence. He may have created in 1363 the bust of a saint in papier-mâché, or rather the marble figure upon which the papier-mâché bust was modeled, for the Church of San Simone. The bust is stylistically very close to the figures of *Solertia*, *Oboedientia*, the Virgin in the *Annunciation* relief, *Virginitas* and also Mary in the depiction of *The Presentation of Christ in the Temple*. The same sculptor probably also created the six reliefs on the baptismal font, dated 1371, in the Florentine Baptistry.

The sculptor of the San Simone bust is unknown, though he may be identifiable as Matteo di Cione, Orcagna's younger brother. We know that Matteo was a professional sculptor. In 1359, he was engaged as his brother's associate in Orvieto, so he may well have been among the sculptors chosen by Orcagna to produce the reliefs on the socle. Of Matteo di Cione we know only that he was matriculated on July 7, 1357 in the stone masons' guild; that he was with Orcagna in Orvieto in 1359; and that he was an heir, together with his brothers Andrea and Jacopo, of Nardo di Cione in 1366; that he was engaged in an unspecified project at Orsanmichele in 1380, and the supplier of marble for the Florence cathedral workshop in 1383; and finally that he died before March 3, 1390, when Jacopo di Cione was sent to Pisa in Matteo's place, to bring a shipment of marble back to Florence. Unfortunately, Matteo's individual works are undocumented, so his connection with the reliefs on the socle of the tabernacle is purely hypothetical.

The half-length figure of *Prudentia* is remarkable for the emotionality suggested by the position of her head, body, and arms, which with great mobility and spatial freedom almost break out of the frame. From a frontal stance, the upper body and shoulders turn in a broad diagonal so that the head is in profile, and thus both of her faces—young in front and old in back—are visible. Both are characterized by deeply-cut eye sockets, rounded cheeks, a powerful, prominent nose, a slight depression around the lips and an aggressive chin; most remarkable are the huge eyes, whose irises and pupils are sharply cut to give them an intense stare. The comparison of *Prudentia* with St. Anne in the relief of the *Birth of the Virgin* indicates that the same sculptor executed the birth relief, following Orcagna's detailed design, of course. Unquestionably, the reliefs of Tobias, the patriarch with his right hand on his lips, the Virtue *Docilitas*, and the prophet pointing to the *Death of the Virgin* stylistically belong to the same group.

In analyzing the style of the tabernacle sculptures, we must remember that the master sculptors hired for this project were guided by Orcagna's designs. Even bearing this in mind, it is almost certain that the sculptor who carved the reliefs listed above also produced the figure of Mary in the *Annunciation of the Death of the Virgin* over the Porta dei Cornacchini of the cathedral of Florence. These sculptures—to which the statue of the Virgin in the *Death Annunciation* and the six reliefs on the socle stand stylistically closest—are surely the work of Alberto Arnoldi. The evidence for this attribution can be found by comparing the reliefs in the group with the forms and cutting of the reliefs firmly documented as by Arnoldi on the Loggia del Bigallo (1361), and in the lunette over the portal of the adjacent Oratorio del Bigallo. Such a comparison strongly suggests that the reliefs of *Prudentia*, the *Birth of the Virgin*, *Tobias*, the patriarch, *Docilitas*, and the prophet on Orcagna's tabernacle were chiseled by Alberto Arnoldi, after Orcagna's designs.

ANOTHER MEMBER OF THE WORKSHOP

The remaining eight reliefs on the socle were executed by another coworker: the *Presentation of the Virgin in the Temple*, the *Marriage of the Virgin*, *Perseverantia*, the *Nativity*, the *Adoration of the Magi*, *Humilitas*, and the two reliefs of a man between leaf tendrils, to the left and right of the pointing prophet directly below the relief of the *Death of the Virgin*. The compositions, the posture and gestures of the figures, the draping of their garments—all these were certainly based on Orcagna's designs, although the sculptor plainly had some difficulty in maintaining their high standard, as a careful examination reveals. The different heads and faces in the pictorial reliefs are unevenly formed, as are the figures of Joachim, Anne, and the high priest in the relief of the *Presentation of the Virgin in the Temple*. The work has been coarsely executed; the features and the hair are scarcely articulated. The hands of Joachim and Anne are too small, and Anne's arms are not in proportion to her body. This is also true in the *Marriage* relief, where the hands are not only too small, but also, in the case of Joseph, rather deformed, as if arthritic. One disappointed suitor, breaking his rod with his right foot, seems to be supported by his (suspended!) left foot. In the case of the other rejected suitor, it is unclear how his raised arm and his head are supposed to go together. In Orcagna's own work there is no such weakness. Mary's face in the *Marriage* relief and that of *Perseverantia* resemble each other strongly, suggesting that they are by the same sculptor. In the *Nativity* relief, the hands of both Mary and Joseph are deformed in the same way as that of Joseph in the *Marriage* relief. Joseph's left hand appears cut off from his arm, and the figures of the angel and shepherd are clumsy. The angel's hair is, as is Joseph's, notched coarsely and mechanically—exactly as is the king's hair in the *Adoration* relief. There, the kings resemble Joseph in the relief of the *Nativity*, as do the Madonna figures in both reliefs and the figure of *Humilitas*. The twin reliefs of a man holding two tendrils resemble the male figures with the kings in the *Adoration*, with Joseph in the *Nativity*, and with the high priest in the *Marriage* scene.

This lack of stylistic balance is a characteristic of this sculptor; another is his awkward comprehension of the organic structure of the human body. Still, Orcagna's detailed designs must have helped him to attain some quality, in spite of these faults. Although this sculptor's presentation of the human figures is weak, he was a master of marble cutting technique, capable of creating figures and scenes from a single block.

Besides Orcagna and the coworkers identified here (Matteo di Cione and Alberto Arnoldi), documents indicate that other gifted figure-sculptors were at work in Florence during the 1350s, notably Francesco Talenti, his son, Simone, and Francesco Neri Ubaldi (Sellaio). Francesco Talenti is not likely to have participated in the tabernacle project; Talenti was Master Builder of the cathedral and there a competitor of Orcagna's; his son, Simone, worked in an entirely different style than that of the reliefs under discussion. During 1362/67 and 1376/77, Sellaio produced fourteen of the sixteen statuettes for the doorposts of the main portal in the cathedral of Florence; his work exhibits all of the above-mentioned characteristics. And so, despite some reservations, he should be considered as a possible participant in the tabernacle work.

ORIGIN AND ARTISTIC SIGNIFICANCE

From the very beginning, Orcagna was able to persuade the best sculptors in Florence to work with him on the tabernacle. Orcagna himself probably contributed only the *Annunciation of the Death of the Virgin* and the *Death and Assumption of the Virgin*, the most significant sculpture of the program. In this work Orcagna repeatedly demonstrates his ability to integrate a great number of scenes into one large, unified composition. He had already done this in 1344/45 in the fresco of the *Triumph of Death*, the *Last Judgement*, and *Hell* in Santa Croce and again, in 1354/57, in the Strozzi altarpiece in Santa Maria Novella. In both of these projects, separate groups of figures come together in a unified planimetrical arrangement.

Although the reliefs were executed by several sculptors, Orcagna was responsible for all of them, because he had made the designs, as the numerous pairs from the 117 sculptures of the tabernacle illustrate. The reliefs cannot be arranged chronologically from less to more spacious compositions, from less to more corporeal figures, or from a "draftsmanlike style" to a "plastic style." On the contrary, they are stylistically homogeneous, probably because Orcagna worked on the designs in a relatively short period of time around 1352. The differences in the more draftsmanlike and the more plastic of these reliefs are the result of different sculptors having worked on them. Orcagna's

Strozzi altarpiece and his reliefs on the tabernacle—particularly the *Presentation of the Virgin in the Temple*—are often thought of as a return to Dugento forms, because of their flatness, their axiality, and the inflexible triangular structure of the composition. This view, however, overlooks certain suggestions of pictorial space, which are essential for an understanding of Orcagna's work. The planimetrical arrangement of the *Presentation of the Virgin in the Temple*, for example, is counteracted by the space implied in the reduction of the figures from front to rear. The ceremonious axiality and triangular structure in the composition, are intended to illustrate a prescribed content, that is to express the divine or the sacerdotal in the scene.

One of Orcagna's greatest artistic achievements is that he attained a successful synthesis of surface and space, both in the Strozzi altarpiece and in the tabernacle reliefs. At the same time, the depicted space acquired a greater depth and, above all, an independence not seen in earlier reliefs, wherein space was created solely by the volume of the figures and objects. Orcagna thus introduced a new stage in Trecento Florentine sculpture, which would lead eventually to Ghiberti's Baptistry door reliefs at the beginning of the Renaissance.

Orcagna's sculptures are among many elements of the extremely rich decoration covering the tabernacle; in addition to the figurative sculptures are variously formed frame profiles and cornices, sculptured foliage and seashells, inlays made of opaque stained glass, and ornamental glass paintings. The play of light and shadow on the sculptured decoration, the multiple colors of the inlays, and the brilliance of the glass surfaces combine to create an overwhelming effect on the viewer. To achieve this, Orcagna developed a decorative style of the highest order, as a comparison with the marble facing on the side-aisle walls (1331) of the cathedral of Florence attests. Francesco Talenti, who directed the cathedral workshop, gave the decoration a greater opulence by a closer setting of the inlays, as can be seen in his work on both western nave aisle doors, the Porta del Campanile, and the Porta dei Cornacchini. Orcagna, however, not only surpassed the diversity and opulence of Talenti's planar decoration, he ushered in a fundamental change by assigning a dominant role to sculpture and sculptural ornament. He thus developed the essentially flat decorative manner begun by Arnolfo di Cambio on the cathedral façade (ca. 1300) with Cosmati-like inlay-work and a profusion of sculpture. With this conceptual change from a dominant flatness to a predominantly sculptural treatment, Orcagna initiated the decorative style of the second half of the fourteenth century.

Overleaf: Detail of the prophet below the relief of the *Death and Assumption of the Virgin* on the east wall *(see plate 94).*

THE PLATES

59

PLATE 4 (*right*):
A zither-playing angel from
the stone frame of the miraculous Madonna.

PLATE 5 (*far right*):
Inlaid spiral colonnettes and
angels on the frame of the
miraculous Madonna.

62

PLATE 6 (*left*):
An angel with a shield and a
cudgel, from the southeast
corner pier.

PLATE 7 (*above*):
King David with his harp,
from the cycle of the Ancestors of Christ on the frieze
over the arcades. This figure
is set directly above the
center of the relief of the
Assumption of the Virgin.

PLATE 8 (*left*):
The Apostle John the Divine, from the southeastern corner pier, displaying the words: *Passus sub Pontio Pilato, crucifixus, mortuus et sepultus* ("He suffered under Pontius Pilate, was crucified, dead and buried") from the Apostles' Creed.

PLATE 9 (*far left*):
The youthful Apostle Thomas from the southeast corner pier. His scroll is inscribed: *Descendit ad inferos, tertia die resurrexit a mortuis* ("He descended into Hell; on the third day he rose again from the dead"), from the Apostles' Creed.

PLATE 10 (*overleaf, left*):
The Apostle Philip, from the northeast corner pier. His blank scroll should read: *Inde venturus est iudicare vivos et mortuos* ("From thence he shall come to judge the living and the dead").

PLATE 11 (*overleaf, right*):
The Apostle Bartholomew, from the northeast corner pier, carrying a book inscribed with the passage: *Credo in Spiritum Sanctum* ("I believe in the Holy Spirit"), his portion of the Apostles' Creed.

67

PLATE 13 (*right*):
Head of an attendant, from the *Birth of the Virgin*.

PLATE 14 (*left*):
Head of an attendant, from
the *Birth of the Virgin*.

PLATE 15 (*above*):
The midwife swaddling the
newborn Mary, from the *Birth
of the Virgin*.

PLATE 16 (*below*):
The *Presentation of the Virgin in the Temple*, from the north socle. Mary, now three years old, is brought to the Temple by her parents, Joachim and Anne, to be dedicated to the service of God.

PLATES 17–21
(*right and following pages*):
Details from the *Presentation of the Virgin in the Temple*.

PLATE 22 (*left*):
Disappointed suitors, from
the *Marriage of the Virgin*.

PLATE 23 (*below*):
The *Marriage of the Virgin*,
from the west socle. Mary,
now twelve years old, is
married to Joseph.

PLATES 24–27
(*following pages*):
Details from the *Marriage of
the Virgin*.

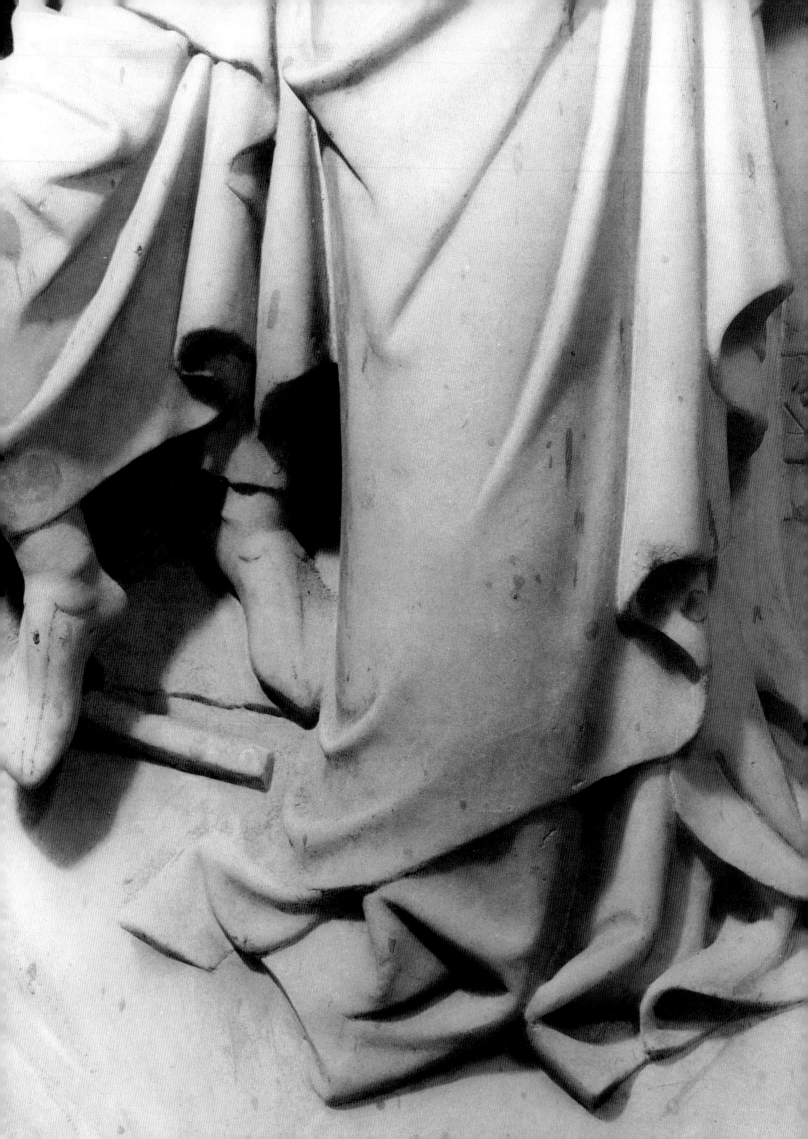

PLATE 28 (*below*):
The *Annunciation*, from the
west socle. Gabriel appears
to Mary, who is shown ab-
sorbed in her books, to tell
her that she will become the
mother of Christ. The Holy
Ghost, in the form of a dove,
carries the incarnation to her.

PLATE 29 (*right*):
Mary, from the *Annuncia-
tion*. Inscribed in her book
are the words ECCE ANCILLA
("Behold the handmaid").

PLATES 30–31 *(overleaf):*
Details from the *Annunciation*.

PLATE 32 (*below*):
The *Nativity*, from the south
socle, combines two events,
the Holy Family at the manger, and the appearance of
the angels to the shepherds.
Mary's position on the ground
expresses her humility.

PLATE 33 (*right*):
Joseph from the *Nativity*.

PLATE 34 (left):
Joseph from the *Nativity*.

PLATE 35 (above):
The Christ Child, from the
Nativity.

PLATE 36 (*left*):
Detail of the eldest magus
kissing the Christ Child's foot,
from the *Adoration of the
Magi*.

PLATE 37 (*below*):
The *Adoration of the Magi*,
from the south socle.

PLATES 38–39 (*overleaf*):
Details of the two younger
kings, from the *Adoration of
the Magi*.

PLATES 41–43
(*right and overleaf*):
Details from the *Presentation of Christ in the Temple*.

PLATE 44 (right):
The *Annunciation of the Death of the Virgin*, from the east socle. Mary, grieving for the loss of her son, is visited again by an angel, carrying a palm from paradise, who tells her that in three days she will be dead. Mary again accepts the will of God, asking only that she be allowed to die in the company of the Apostles.

PLATES 45–47
(far right and overleaf):
Details from the *Annunciation of the Death of the Virgin*.

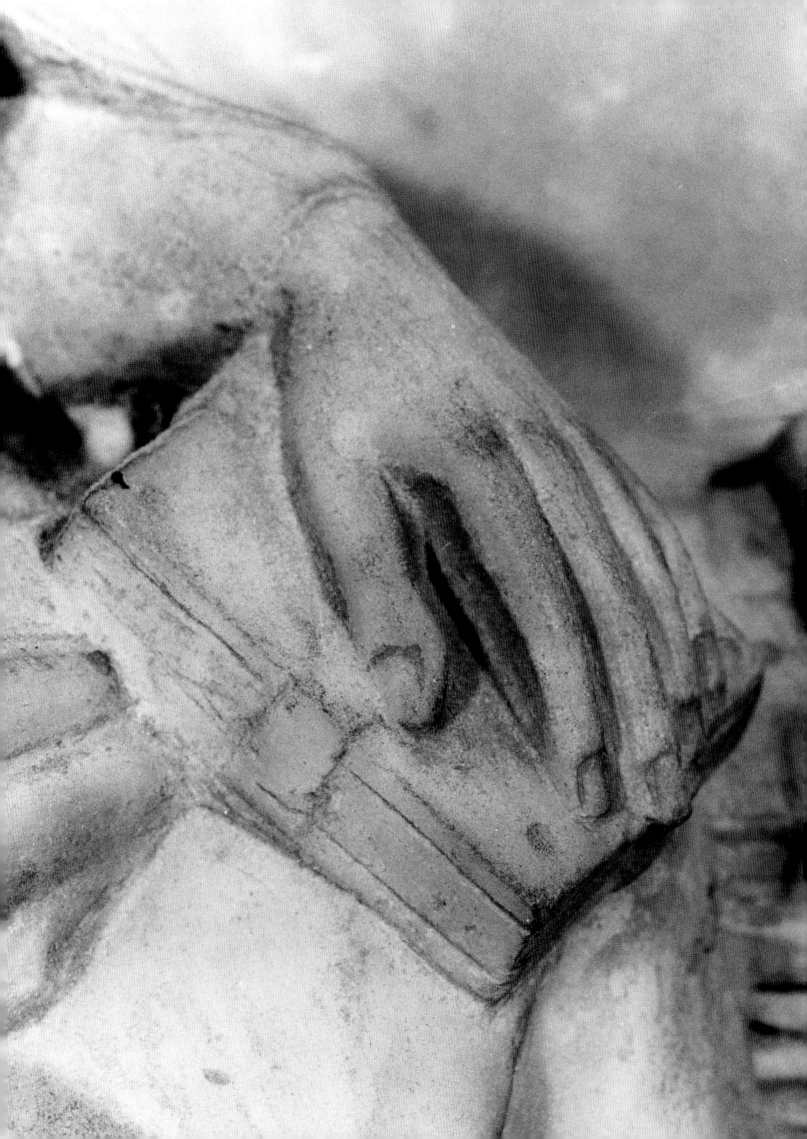

PLATE 48 (*opposite*):
The *Death and Assumption
of the Virgin*, from the east
wall, a double relief culmi-
nating the Marian cycle. The
lower register portrays Mary's
death as a fourteenth-century
funeral, with the Apostles,
who have been miraculously
assembled at the Virgin's last
request, appearing as mourn-
ers. Christ, accompanied by
a retinue of saints and angels
from heaven, cradles Mary's
soul on his left arm. According to Vasari, Orcagna's sixteenth-century biographer,
the man in the turban-like
kerchief in the second row
at the far right *(plate 57)* is
a portrait of the artist. In the
upper register Mary is carried to heaven by angels.
She drops her belt into the
hands of Saint Thomas, to
allay his doubts about the
truth of the miracle.

PLATES 49–58
(*near left and following pages*):
Details from the *Death and
Assumption of the Virgin*.

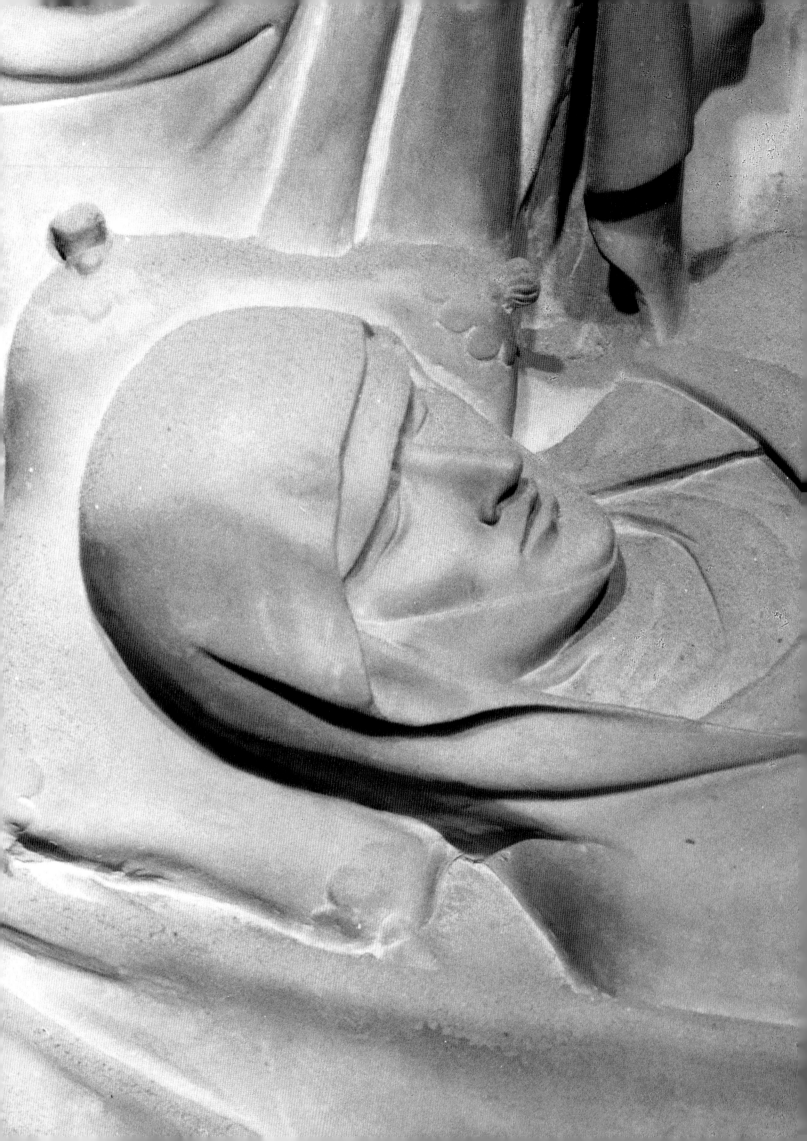

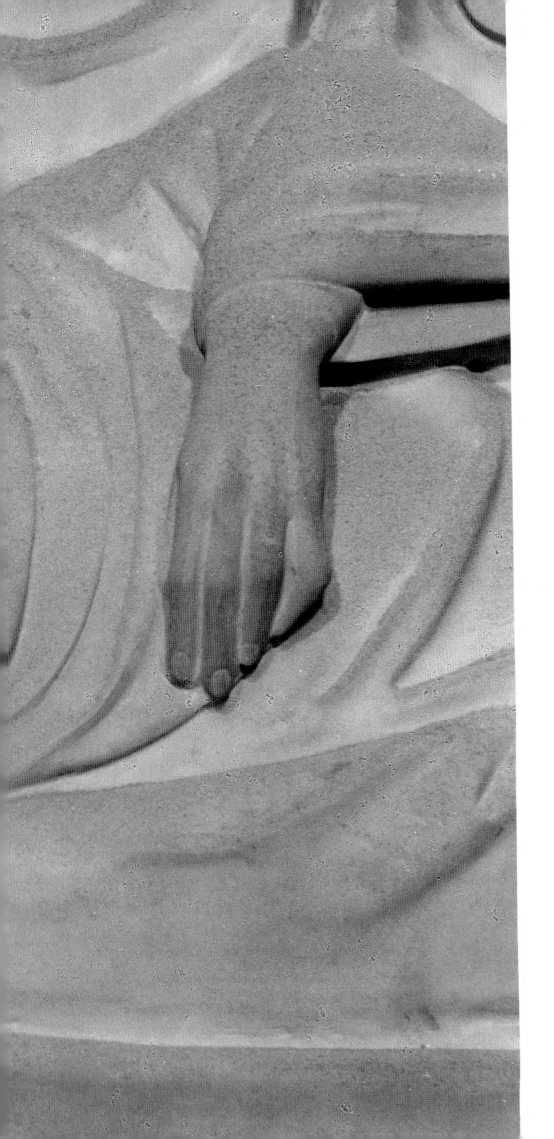

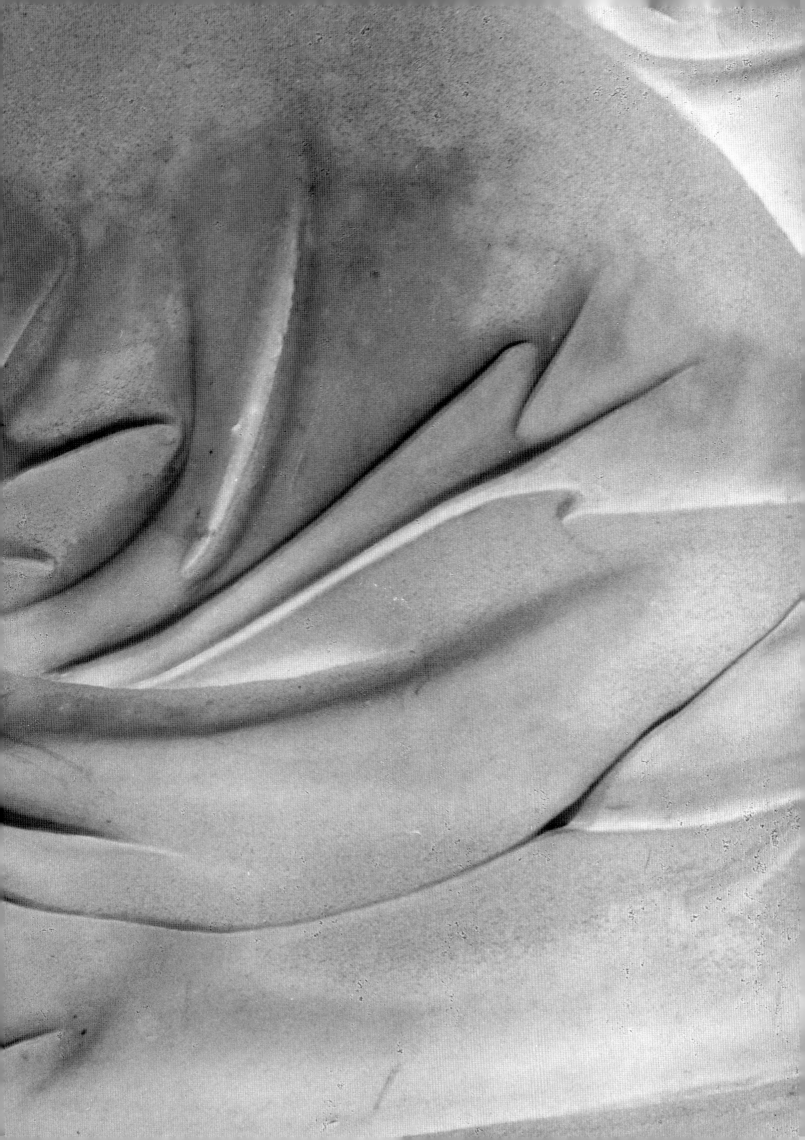

PLATE 57 *(near right):*
Mourner from the *Death of*
the Virgin, said by Vasari,
Orcagna's sixteenth-century
biographer, to be a portrait
of the artist.

PLATE 59:
Fides (Faith), from the north socle. The first of the three Theological Virtues, Faith, Hope, and Charity, listed by St. Paul in I Corinthians 13:13, *Fides* is shown as a confident figure, firm in her belief in God. She holds a cup covered with a paten in her right hand and a cross, now broken off, in her left.

PLATE 60:
Spes (Hope), from the west
socle. The second of the
Theological Virtues, Hope
personifies the Christian desire
for spiritual perfection. Her
act of reaching for the floating crown represents the
aspiration for eternal life.

PLATE 61 (*right*):
Caritas (Love or Charity), from the south socle. The third and greatest of the Theological Virtues, *Caritas* is shown as a mother nursing a child, a symbol of the Christian love of humanity. Her flaming crown and the burning heart in her left hand represent the love of God. As the nurturing mother of Christ and the intercessor for mankind, Mary was thought to personify this virtue particularly.

PLATES 62–64
(far right and overleaf):
Details of the nursing child and the head of *Caritas*.

PLATE 65 (*right*):
View of the northeastern corner pier, showing an unidentified male figure, probably a prophet, facing the relief of the *Birth of the Virgin* on the north socle. Behind him, shown obliquely, is the virtue *Solertia* (Ingenuity), in an attitude of intense reflection.

PLATE 66 (*far right*):
Detail of the head of *Prudentia*, from the northeastern corner pier.

PLATE 67 (*far left*):
The left hand of *Prudentia*, crushing a snake.

PLATE 68 (*left*):
The Cardinal Virtue *Prudentia* (Prudence), from the northeastern corner pier. The four Cardinal Virtues Prudence, Justice, Fortitude, and Temperance were enumerated by Plato, and later taken into the Christian canon by medieval theologians. *Prudentia* is shown with two faces, an older one gazing backward into the past, and thus learning from experience, and a younger one looking forward into the future. With her left hand she crushes a snake, symbolizing evil, a demonstration that Wisdom can overcome the mere cunning of wickedness.

PLATES 69–70 (*overleaf*):
Details of *Solertia* (Ingenuity) and *Docilitas* (Erudition), two virtues associated with *Prudentia*, from the southeastern corner pier.

129

PLATES 71–72:
Two unidentified figures,
probably prophets, from the
northeastern corner pier.

PLATE 74 (*right*):
Detail of the head of *Justitia*.

PLATE 75 *(right):*
Devotio (Devotion), a virtue
associated with *Justitia*, from
the northwestern corner pier.

PLATE 76 *(overleaf, left):*
Detail of *Oboedientia* (Obedience), another virtue associated with *Justitia*, from
the northwestern corner pier.

PLATE 77 *(overleaf, right):*
Detail of the Biblical hero
Tobias, from the northwest-
ern corner pier.

PLATE 78 *(right):*
View of the northwestern corner pier, showing the Evangelist Luke, gesturing toward the nearby relief of the *Marriage of the Virgin*, and behind him, the virtue *Devotio*.

PLATE 79 *(far right):*
Detail of the head of Luke.

PLATE 84 *(above):*
An unidentified prophet, from
the southwestern corner pier.

PLATE 85 *(right):*
An unidentified patriarch,
from the southwestern corner
pier.

PLATE 86 *(right):*
The Cardinal Virtue *Tem-perantia* (Temperance), from
the southeastern corner pier.
She is shown holding a compass, reflecting her careful,
measuring character.

PLATES 87–89
(far right and overleaf):
Details of *Temperantia*.

PLATE 90
(second overleaf, left):
Detail of *Virginitas* (Virginity), a virtue associated with
Temperantia, from the southeastern corner pier.

PLATE 91
(second overleaf, right):
Detail of *Humilitas* (Humility), another virtue associated with *Temperantia*, from
the southeastern corner pier.
According to St. Thomas
Aquinas, Humility, one of
the most important attri-
butes of Mary, was the first
step on the pathway to God.

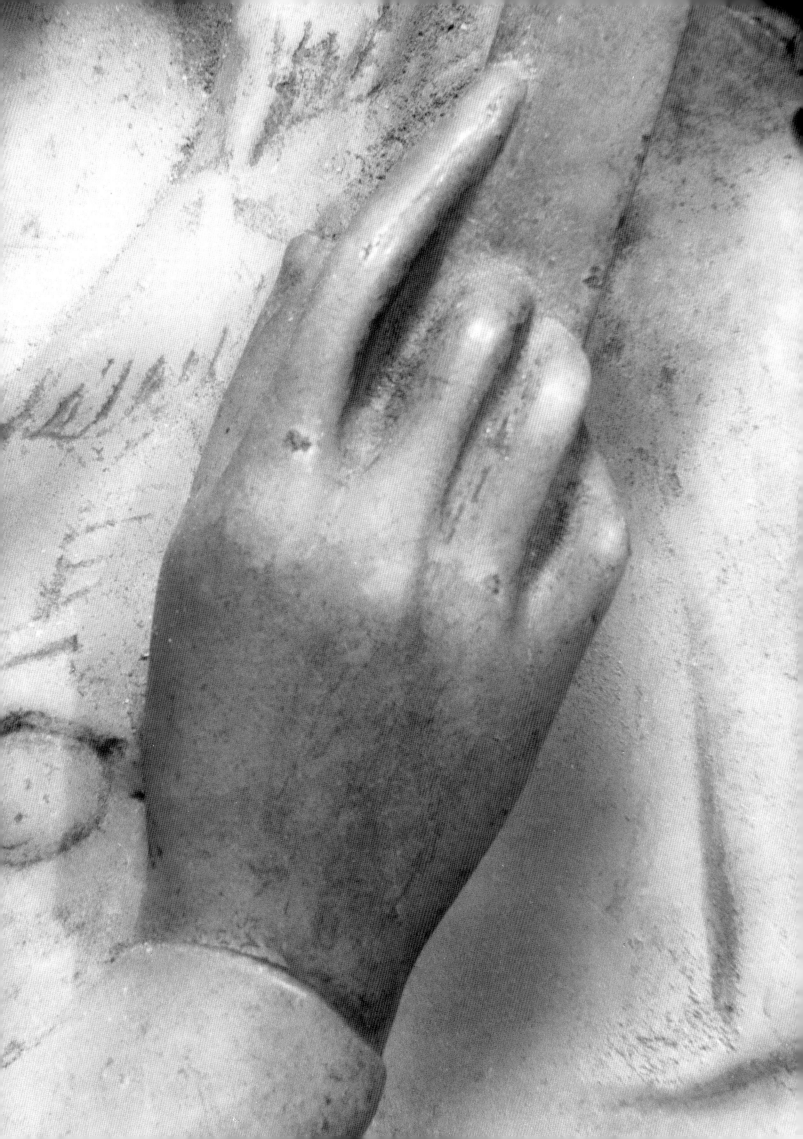

PLATE 92
(previous spread, left):
Detail of an unidentified
prophet or apostle from the
southeastern corner pier.

PLATE 93
(previous spread, right):
Detail of an unidentified
patriarch or priest from the
southeastern corner pier.

PLATE 94 *(above):*
Unidentified prophet below
the relief of the *Death and
Assumption of the Virgin* on
the east wall.

PLATE 95 *(above)*:
Tendril with baby's head,
growing from the body of a
seated male figure below the
*Death and Assumption of the
Virgin* relief on the east wall.

COMMENTARIES ON THE PLATES

THE BIRTH OF THE VIRGIN

The literary sources for Mary's birth, the *Gospel According to St. James*, the apocryphal *Gospel of St. Matthew*, or the *Golden Legend* by Jacopo da Voragine did not provide concrete direction to the artist. The *Golden Legend* relates that Joachim and Anne, as predetermined, met at the Golden Gate in the city walls of Jerusalem. They rejoiced at the promise of a child that would be sent to them, and after they had praised God, they went home. And so Anne bore a daughter, called Mary.

Orcagna placed the *Birth of the Virgin* in a faithfully depicted Gothic bedroom, an alcove whose curtains are drawn apart. Anne lies on the bed, her left arm stretched forward as she props up her head with her right hand; she bends slightly forward, so she can gently stroke the head of Mary, who is held by a midwife over a wash basin. The midwife's helper, holding a bowl and pitcher, stands behind the bed, while at its foot two women converse about Mary. To illustrate the emotional quality of the relationship of mother and child, and the spatial gradation of the figures, Orcagna was no doubt inspired by Giotto's paintings. Pietro Lorenzetti's triptych of the *Birth of the Virgin*, created in 1342 for an altar in the Siena cathedral, may have influenced his realistic arrangement of the interior space, and perhaps also suggested the motif of the drawn curtain.

THE PRESENTATION OF THE VIRGIN IN THE TEMPLE

When Mary, in the *Gospel According to St. James* and other sources, was three years old, Joachim and Anne brought her to the temple, as agreed, to give her as an offering to the priests. Mary did not turn back toward her parents as she climbed up the fifteen steps to the temple. This unchildlike behavior was a sign that Mary was aware of her special destiny. The priest received the child, kissed her and blessed her with these words: "The Lord has made your name great among all generations; in you the Lord will manifest his redemption for the sons of Israel at the end of time!"

In his relief of the *Presentation of the Virgin in the Temple*, Orcagna does not stage the scene in front of the temple as a whole, as did Taddeo Gaddi in the Baroncelli chapel, but rather as a frontal view of the temple's entrance. Above a high foundation, at the center of the building, is an open gate, on both sides of which is a gallery. Leading to the temple's portals—as described in the apocryphal *Gospel of St. Matthew*—are fifteen steps. Exactly midway up the staircase stands the childlike figure of Mary, whose face and right forearm are broken off. Nevertheless, it is obvious that Mary, contrary to the literary source, but in agreement with Taddeo Gaddi's depiction, is turning around on this step so that one may see her full face. As Mary twists around, her left arm seems to point away while her right arm points forward to the high priest who, accompanied by two men, waits under the portal to receive the Virgin. In the side galleries, two handmaidens in various attitudes, one of them seem-

Opposite: The tabernacle of the miraculous Madonna.

ingly curious, await her. Kneeling to the right and left of the staircase are Mary's parents, Joachim and Anne. Orcagna sharply differentiates the spatial planes, near and distant, with strikingly different figures: in the foreground, Joachim, Mary, and Anne; in the background, the smaller high priest and the handmaidens. Orcagna knowingly avoided inflexibility in the composition by establishing not one plane, but two, which constantly interpenetrate. This device creates a seldom achieved balance between the space and the planimetry of the relief.

The significance of the curtain, which is gathered up at the sides of the *Presentation* relief, is unclear. To interpret it as a sort of theater curtain would be anachronistic. It may allude to the medieval custom of veiling and unveiling religious pictures, as was done with the miracle-working Madonna in Orsanmichele.

THE MARRIAGE OF THE VIRGIN

The *Gospel According to St. James*, and other sources, report that Mary was enclosed in the temple like a dove and received nourishment from the hand of an angel. When she was twelve years old, there was a discussion among the priests: "Now that Mary has turned twelve years old, what should we do with her so that she will not defile the temple of the Lord?" So they went to the high priest and said: "You stand at the altar of the Lord, go into the sanctuary and pray on her behalf, and we will do whatever it is the Lord demands." The high priest took his amulet with the twelve bells, entered the inner sanctum and prayed on her behalf. An angel of the Lord suddenly stood before him and said to him: "Zacharias, Zacharias, go out and gather the widowers among the population. Each should carry a rod, and to whomever of these the Lord gives a miraculous sign, he shall have her for his wife!" Messengers were dispatched throughout all of Judea; and when the widowers were gathered together, they all took their rods and went to the high priest. He took the rods and went into the temple to pray. After he finished praying, he gathered the rods, and went back out to redistribute them, as he had not received a miraculous sign. The last rod to be given back was Joseph's, and from this rod leaves sprouted and a dove appeared, which then flew onto Joseph's head. Then the high priest said to Joseph, "Joseph, the Lord has chosen you for the Virgin; take her in your guardianship!"

Orcagna centered his composition on the main figures in the story: Joseph with the leaf-sprouting rod which signifies that he has been chosen, and Mary, both in profile; between them, in frontal view, is the high priest. The couple behind Joseph and Mary are marriage witnesses, and the two figures behind the high priest are his retinue. To the left of this central group are two failed suitors who, vexed by their lack of success in winning Mary, respectively break a dried up rod and raise a fist. The figures of the suitors to the left of Joseph correspond with the empty area on the other side of the central grouping, which acts as a compositional counter-weight. A curtain, which is fastened to the upper four corners of the frame, provides the background for this scene, giving the impression of a canopy. This detail does not appear in any text describing the scene.

THE ANNUNCIATION

According to the *Gospel According to St. James*, Mary was selected to weave a purple curtain for the temple. During this time, she took a jug and went outside to draw water. A voice spoke to her: "Hail, thou who art full of grace, the Lord is with thee; thou art blessed among women." She could not see where the voice came from, and went back, trembling, into the house. There an angel of the Lord stood by her and said: "Fear not, Mary, for thou hast found favor in the sight of God, and thou shalt conceive from his word."

On the left side of Orcagna's relief, the angel Gabriel kneels, holding in his left hand a lily, the symbol of purity, while raising his right hand in greeting and transmittal of the heavenly message; this hand points directly at the dove of the Holy Ghost, who carries the divine incarnation. Orcagna suggests by the fluttering lock of Gabriel's hair that he has just arrived. Mary sits on the right side of the composition, gazing at the angel, her head bent forward, listening, and her arms crossed humbly over her breasts. The book that she was holding upon Gabriel's arrival, now lies open on her knees. The words ECCE ANCILLA are visible. With these words: "Behold, I am the handmaiden of the Lord," Mary answered the angel's announcement, voicing her humility and submission to the will of God. In this depiction, Orcagna was obviously influenced by the *Annunciation* panel (Pinacoteca, Siena) painted by Ambrogio Lorenzetti in 1344 for the tax office of the Palazzo Pubblico in Siena. Instead of Lorenzetti's gold ground, Orcagna has supplied a background of flat blue majolica, which sets off the figures so emphatically that they almost appear free-standing.

THE NATIVITY

The literary source for the depiction of the *Nativity* comes from the *Gospel According to St. Luke* (2:7): "And she brought forth her first-born son, and wrapped him in swaddling clothes, and laid him in a manger; because there was no room for them in the inn."

Orcagna's relief of the *Nativity* combines two scenes: that of the Child in the manger at Bethlehem and, behind it, the annunciation to the shepherds. Mary and Joseph sit on the rocky ground in front of the manger. While Joseph is sunk in sleep, his head propped up by his right hand, Mary leans toward the Child and tenderly readjusts the sheet around him. Only part of his chest and his head are uncovered. The left hand which the Child has brought up from under the sheet, lies on his chest and points with an outstretched index finger at his mother. The meaning of this gesture, which may have an iconographical significance, is unknown. Behind the manger, the rocky ground graduates into a hill, on which stand an ox and a donkey. An angel floats above the hill. He turns toward the shepherds at the right of the ridge, which rises steeply behind the foremost hill, and points with his right hand toward the Child in the manger. With a dramatic sweep of his left hand he announces the message of the birth of the Redeemer. As in the relief of the *Presentation of the Virgin in the Temple*, the upper four corners of the octagonal frame are draped with a drawn curtain. Here, too, the curtain may signify the unveiling of a holy image. One particularly important detail of this relief should be noted: Mary does not lie beside the manger or kneel before the Child, but rather sits next to him on the rocky ground. This is especially remarkable, since in the following relief of the *Adoration of the Magi*, which also takes place in Bethlehem, Mary and the Child are enthroned under a baldachin. This setting directly follows the example of Taddeo Gaddi's fresco of the same scene in the Baroncelli chapel (ca. 1330/33), where Mary is shown sitting on the ground with the Child on her arm. Taddeo Gaddi's fresco (as also in the *Annunciation* in the same cycle), develops the motif of the "Madonna of Humility," a type evidently introduced by Simone Martini, in the fresco on the lunette of the portal of Notre Dame-des-Doms in Avignon (ca. 1340/43). Sitting on the ground is an expression of Mary's humility, which, along with her motherhood, qualifies her to act as mediator for the Redeemer of the World, protecting the Child in the manger. In Orcagna's relief, Mary's importance is communicated by the Child's strict frontality and by his hand gesture.

THE ADORATION OF THE MAGI

According to the description of the Epiphany in the *Golden Legend*, on the day of the Lord's birth, there appeared to three kings, or magi, a star in the shape of a beautiful child with a shining cross over its head. The star spoke to the kings: "Go immediately to the land of Judah, where you will find the newborn king that you seek." The star in the shape of a child can be seen in Orcagna's relief over the canopy, where the Christ Child, seated in the lap of the enthroned Virgin, receives the homage of the three kings. Mary sits on a high throne at the left of the relief, facing right, to gaze at the kings; in a similar posture the Christ Child sits on her knee. He leans slightly forward, and in a gesture of blessing, lays his right hand against the forehead of the oldest king, who kneels before him, kissing his foot; the King has taken off his crown and placed it next to him on the ground. Behind the first king stand the other two, one middle-aged, the other youthful; they turn to one another in conversation, the middle-aged one raising his arm, apparently pointing at the star, which led them to Christ. Orcagna illustrates Christ's kingship by removing the scene from the manger stall, and placing Mary and Christ under a festive canopy in a chair of state. According to the *Golden Legend* the kings' gifts of gold, incense, and myrrh signify "gold as a tribute, because he—Christ—was the highest king; incense as an offering because he was God; myrrh for a funeral, because he was mortal."

PRESENTATION OF CHRIST IN THE TEMPLE

Orcagna's relief of the *Presentation of Christ in the Temple* is based on the *Gospel According to St. Luke* (2:22–39): "And when the days of her purification according to the law of Moses were accomplished, they brought him to Jerusalem, to present him to the Lord." St. Luke's account, which describes the two ceremonies as occurring at the same time, does not correspond with the practice prescribed by Mosaic law. Forty days were to pass between childbirth and the day the mother might come to the Temple for Purification, whereas the ceremony known as Presentation took place thirty days after a child's birth. In the Presentation ceremony, the father presented his first-born son to the priest and subsequently redeemed him for five shekels. The rites of Purification, however, insisted that a lamb or two doves be brought for a burnt offering. According to St. Luke (2:25–35), the Holy Ghost revealed to Simeon, a pious man in Jerusalem, that before his death, he would see Christ. He came to the temple at the right moment to take Christ, whom he recognized as the anticipated Redeemer, in his arms. Similarly, an old prophetess, Anna, "coming in that instant gave thanks likewise unto the Lord, and spake of him to all them that looked for redemption in Jerusalem" (St. Luke, 2:38). This exact phrase is inscribed on Anna's scroll in Ambrogio Lorenzetti's polyptych painted in 1342 for the cathedral in Siena (Uffizi, Florence), which depicts the *Presentation* and the *Purification*. In the foreground of Ambrogio's panel is the meeting of Joseph and Mary with Simeon and Anna, and in the background—although central, nevertheless understated—is the high priest with the dove-offering for purification. A similar treatment of both scenes appears in Taddeo Gaddi's small panel (Museo dell'Accademia, Florence), which was painted for a sacristy cabinet for the Florentine Franciscans.

The *Golden Legend* relates that Mary, because of the virgin birth, was not required to undergo purification, but she did so anyway out of respect for the law. Presumably for this reason, Giotto, in his fresco of the *Presentation* in the Scrovegni chapel in Padua (ca. 1305), gave no trace of the rite, limiting his narrative to the meeting with Simeon and Anna. Jacopo del Casentino followed Giotto's example in a panel painted around 1330 (Collection of G. Salvadori, Florence), but did include a flame at the altar as an allusion to the ceremony. Mary's purification was more emphatically suggested by Taddeo Gaddi and Ambrogio Lorenzetti, by the inclusion of the figure of the high priest.

Orcagna's relief signifies a new reflection of the theme. His scene is set in an interior with three walls that are arranged to form a hexagonal vault. In the center of this space is a hexagonal altar, with a fire for the burnt offering. Around this altar stand the Virgin to the left, the aged Simeon with the Child in his arms in the middle, and the prophetess Anna and Joseph (carrying two doves) to the right. In contrast to Jacopo del Casentino's panel, where the purification is only hinted at by the fire and the pair of doves, and to Taddeo Gaddi's and Ambrogio Lorenzetti's paintings, which include the high priest, Orcagna's relief depicts the meeting of Mary and the Child with Simeon and Anna, who both recognize the hoped-for Redeemer. The relief thus emphasizes the Christ Child's identity as the Messiah.

ANNUNCIATION OF THE DEATH OF THE VIRGIN

Orcagna now takes a great leap forward in his cycle of the Life of Mary in the following scene, which shows the *Annunciation of the Death of the Virgin*. According to the *Golden Legend* of Jacopo da Voragine, "One day, when Mary longed so to see her son again that she could not restrain her tears, an angel appeared before her and announced that within three days she would be dead; he brought her a palm from paradise, which was to be placed on her bier." Orcagna shows a Gothic room, as realistic as the alcove in the relief of the *Birth of the Virgin*. Along the left wall and the entire rear wall stands a wooden bench with an armrest at each end and a high back. On the rear wall, over the bench, is a window, whose position at the left part of the wall suggests that there is a second window in a corresponding position at the right, but which is blocked by the appearance of the angel. Mary sits on the bench in front of the left wall. On the seat beside her, in front of the rear wall, three books lie in disorder, indicating their recent use. Simultaneously Mary lets the book in her left hand drop to her knee, and raising her right hand in greeting or alarm at the startling news, gazes up at the angel. Opposite Mary, the angel floats slightly above her in front of the right wall, and leaning forward, faces the Virgin as if in intense dialogue with her. The curtain in this scene differs from that in the other reliefs in the cycle; here, the cloth resembles the chiseled drapery with which Orcagna has surrounded Bernardo Daddi's miraculous image.

The two last scenes of the cycle of the Life of Mary, the *Death and Assumption of the Virgin*, are depicted in a uniquely monumental way, where one scene is set off by the other. The size of this relief, set on the wall of the rear arch opposite the back of the miraculous image, suggests that these scenes are the culmination of the entire cycle. Mary's death is shown as the first stage and prerequisite to her glorification and Assumption. When the angel, according to the story in the *Golden Legend*, announced her death, Mary asked to die in the circle of the apostles. So John, who was already preaching in Ephesus, was conveyed by a white cloud to Mary's house, as were the other apostles. When Mary saw them all gathered together, she praised the Lord and sat among them. At the third hour, Christ arrived with a band of angels, legions of patriarchs, martyrs, and confessors, and a choir of virgins. The entire heavenly host surrounded Mary and began to sing praises. Christ said to her, "Come, I will seat you on my throne, because I wish your presence." Mary answered, "Lord, my soul is ready." Thereupon Mary's soul left her body and was taken up in Christ's arms.

This detailed description makes Orcagna's depiction comprehensible: Mary lies, just deceased, stretched out on her deathbed on a bier cloth, which is held at either end by an apostle. Mary's folded left arm rests on her breast, while an apostle behind the bed bends over to kiss her outstretched right hand. In the center, behind the bed, stands Christ, who holds Mary's soul in the form of a small figure on his left arm, while his right arm is stretched out toward her body. Christ is surrounded by angels, two of whom carry large candles, as was the custom at funerals in the fourteenth century. The angels are crowned with diadems. Thanks to the *Golden Legend*, the rest of the group can be identified: the six men in togas standing on either side of Christ in front of the death bed, grieving and lamenting, are probably apostles. In the center of the group, to the left of the bed, standing behind an apostle, near the head of Mary, a man, whose priestly rank is identified by his stola, holds an open book in both hands and reads from it. He is escorted by two angels on either side, who carry his stola; the foremost angel in his left hand carries a censer, whose burning incense signifies an ascending prayer. This trio is obviously engaged in praying for the dead Virgin. Both bearded men to the rear may be patriarchs, who are mentioned in the *Golden Legend*. Behind the apostles at the head of the bed, there is also a group of virgins in Christ's retinue. The figures at the right section of the relief, behind the apostle holding the bier cloth, represent the legions of patriarchs, martyrs, and confessors. Among them, two men are deeply engaged in conversation; their gestures suggest that they are talking about what has just taken place. The man to the right, whose head is somewhat larger than those of the other figures, stands out by his unusually lively, individualistic features; as mentioned earlier, Vasari identified this head as a portrait of Orcagna.

In his composition of the *Death of the Virgin*, Orcagna confined himself to the pictorial tradition followed by sculptors since the 12th century, after the miniaturists of the 10th and 11th centuries, who in their turn were inspired by Byzantine ivory work. The placing of numerous figures about Mary's deathbed may have been directly influenced by the *Golden Legend*. But contrary to this literary source, Orcagna's heavenly band are not assembled to sing songs of praise; they are there for a funeral. The large candles that the angels are carrying are suitable for a burial ceremony, as are the group of praying celebrants and the two angels with the censer. Moreover, Orcagna has given Mary's deathbed the form of a sarcophagus. Finally, the gesture which Christ makes with his left arm creates distance between the corpse and the soul. Thus, while depicting the *Death of the Virgin*, Orcagna evokes the idea of Mary's burial, which will be counteracted by her Assumption.

The *Golden Legend* reports that upon Mary's death, the Lord instructed the apostles to place her body in a newly dug grave in the valley of Josaphat and to wait three days for his return. The apostles did as they were told. After three days the Lord appeared to them and asked the apostles what honor would be suitable for the glory of the Mother of God. They answered that as the Lord himself had overcome death, so also the body of his mother should be resurrected, and that she should sit at his right side in eternal glory. Immediately Mary's soul, unified with her body, ascended with a band of angels to heaven. Thomas, as the *Golden Legend* indicates, was not there when the incident occurred, and refused to believe in Mary's Assumption. So the Virgin's girdle, intact and still knotted, fell down into his hand, whereupon the doubter knew that the Virgin's body must have indeed been assumed into heaven.

Orcagna extended a narrow strip of earth or rock across the entire width of the relief to separate the scene of Mary's death from that of her Assumption. Rising from the middle section of this strip is a hill, from which Mary's ascent begins. Mary is enthroned on a cushioned bench, set against a red background decorated with gold stars, within a mandorla. Her feet rest on a pedestal near its point, which is covered by small clouds. Four angels carry the mandorla, while between them float two other angels, playing a trumpet, and a bagpipe. Doubting Thomas kneels at the lower left, looking up at Mary with hands outstretched to receive her girdle, which may have been originally supplied in bronze. In the corner opposite Thomas are three small trees, the middle and largest one being an oak. The background is formed by an inlaid surface, which looks like richly embroidered blue cloth. Such a blue background with inlays may have seemed the equivalent of the gold background of a painting ornamented with punch-work. The blue background contrasts with the red and gold mandorla and its geometrical radiating pattern. Owing to its red color, the mandorla can have no cosmic meaning; it represents the emanation of heavenly light in which Mary is bathed.

Orcagna did not attempt to show Mary rising from the midst of the apostles into heaven. Instead he linked the Assumption theme with that of Thomas receiving the girdle. His intent was to depict the *Assumption* so that the glorification of the Virgin and her bodily acceptance into heaven would seem a concrete reality, and Doubting Thomas's receiving of the girdle would appear as irrefutable evidence of this having happened.

It has been suggested that Orcagna's emphasis on the Assumption relief may reflect the ending of a Milanese siege of Florence in the summer of 1351. This happened in the days immediately before August 15, the feast of the Assumption. The scene's religious meaning would seem the more convincing reason, however: the portrayal of Mary as the Mother of God, whose body ascended into heaven and who acts as Christ's mediator for mankind.

THE THEOLOGICAL VIRTUES

Orcagna has placed each of these three virtues between two scenes of the Life of Mary. Each is personified as a female figure seated on a bench before a background of blue majolica. With this depiction of *Fides*, *Spes*, and *Caritas*, Orcagna followed the example of the virtue cycle on the bronze door of the south portal of the Florentine Baptistery, done by Andrea Pisano during 1330/33. Like those figures, Orcagna's virtues are not shown as winged beings, but rather than having hexagonal halos, they are crowned. Only *Spes* does not wear a crown, but rather tries to grasp one which floats in the air in front of her.

Fides. *Fides* holds a cup covered with a paten in her extended right hand and a (broken off) cross in her left. These attributes refer to the crucifixion of Christ and to the mass. This depiction is close to that of Andrea Pisano on the baptistry door, and also to that of Taddeo Gaddi, painted in 1330/33 in a tondo on the window jamb of the Baroncelli chapel at Santa Croce.

Spes. Turned toward the right, *Spes* sits on her bench, her head in profile. Both arms are extended, with the palms of her hands facing upward, where, attached to the frame of the relief, a crown is floating. The act of trying to grasp the floating crown represents the hope of obtaining eternal life. Here again Orcagna has followed the example of Andrea Pisano, although without equipping his *Spes* with Andrea's "wings of hope." Whereas Giotto painted *Spes* in the Scrovegni chapel in Padua (1303/05) as an erect, floating figure, and Andrea Pisano and Taddeo Gaddi similarly depicted her drawn up from a sitting position through the strength of hope, Orcagna's *Spes* does not, by her posture, indicate a longing for heaven. Her more composed demeanor resembles that of *Spes* from the virtue cycle of the Campanile of Florence's cathedral.

Caritas. Orcagna depicts *Caritas* as a mother nursing a child. She carries a flaming heart in her left hand and wears a flaming crown on her head. Nursing the child is a directly comprehensible symbol of *Caritas proximi*, the active love of one's fellow man and of Christian charity. The flaming heart and crown are symbols of *Caritas dei*, the love of God. Orcagna's depiction resembles the nursing Mary, the Mother of God, who calms the Christ Child. Nicola Pisano carved on his pulpit in Pisa's baptistry (completed 1260) a figure of *Caritas*, as a motherly woman holding a naked child; on his pulpit in the Siena cathedral (1264/67) he gave *Caritas* the attribute of a cornucopia of flames. His son Giovanni Pisano also depicted the nursing mother several times on his pulpit in Pisa Cathedral (1301/10). Following Giovanni Pisano, the Sienese sculptor Tino di Camaino created, around 1322, a statue of *Caritas* (today in the Museo Bardini, Florence) holding two children to her breasts; and Giovanni di Balduccio, for his 1333/34 tabernacle of the miraculous image in Orsanmichele—the predecessor of Orcagna's tabernacle—carved a *Caritas* relief (now in the National Gallery of Art, Washington), in which the figure of the virtue nurses two children from streams emanating from her flaming heart. Giovanni di Balduccio's source for this attribute was Giotto's *Caritas* in the Scrovegni chapel. Thus Giotto's *Caritas* figure combines the love of *Amor proximi* and *Amor dei*. This type was directly taken over by Andrea Pisano, and by Taddeo Gaddi for the arch of the Baroncelli chapel and the virtue cycle in the Campanile of the Florence cathedral. Thus, Orcagna's *Caritas* relief conflates the iconography of Giotto and the Pisan sculptors.

THE RELIEFS ON THE NORTHEASTERN CORNER PIER

Five reliefs adorn the socle of the northeastern corner pier; the Cardinal Virtue, *Prudentia*, located on the corner, is flanked by *Docilitas*

(Erudition) and *Solertia* (Ingenuity), which are presented as half-length female figures. These are joined by two half-length bearded male figures carrying large scrolls, on which text may have been originally painted, but which are now blank; they are figures from the Old or New Testaments, who point to or are turned toward the neighboring scenes of the Life of Mary.

Prudentia. Prudentia is identifiable by the fact that she has two faces, one old, the other young. Her right hand holds a corner of her overgarment; her left hand holds a snake. As with the head of Janus, the old face looks backward into the past and the young face looks steadily at the newly subdued snake, a reference to the snake that tempted Eve in Eden; intelligence overcomes the cunning of the wicked. Orcagna's depiction of *Prudentia* was obviously derived from Andrea Pisano's bronze relief of the same subject.

Docilitas and *Solertia*. There are no examples of the Virtues Erudition and Ingenuity in the expansive virtue cycle in Taddeo Gaddi's Baroncelli chapel. Orcagna and his program advisor seem to have invented their own iconography for these striking representations. Erudition appears as an older woman, whose age indicates experience and wisdom. Over her clothing, a dress and a shawl which covers her head and neck snugly, *Docilitas* wears a cloak lined with fur, except for the hood, the tip of which tilts forward. This costume is unmistakably taken from contemporary professorial dress. A more obvious expression of Erudition is also her hand gesture, with the forefinger of the right hand lying on the crooked small finger of the left hand, a gesture used in the summing up of an argument in a discourse ("and fifthly!"). *Solertia* (Ingenuity), a young woman in a classical hairstyle, places the forefinger of her right hand over her lower lip, seemingly as a sign of intense reflection. In the other hand, she holds a scroll containing her name.

Two male half-length figures. The one on the side of the pier which is adjacent to the beginning of the cycle of the Life of Mary at the north side of the tabernacle, by his posture and gesture draws attention to the scene of the *Birth of the Virgin*. Because his scroll carries no text or name, his identity is uncertain; so is that of the male figure attached to the side of the pier adjacent to the relief of the *Annunciation of the Death of the Virgin*. This fully frontal figure, with his blank scroll, points with his broken off forefinger to the relief beside him.

THE RELIEFS ON THE NORTHWESTERN CORNER PIER

At the corner of this pier, in the socle area, is the relief of *Justitia* (Justice), presenting her customary attributes, the sword and the scale, following Andrea Pisano's depiction of her. In attendance are the half-length female figures of the minor virtues *Oboedientia* (Obedience) and *Devotio* (Devotion), identified on the banderoles; their gestures give no specific reference to their respective qualities. The two half-length male figures on the pier are identified by their chiselled inscriptions as Tobias and Luke.

Justitia. As the Cardinal Virtue identifiable by a crown, *Justitia* holds a sword in her left hand and a scale in her right. The scale indicates the obligation of *Justitia* to balance evidence, and the sword refers to her duty to separate good from evil.

Oboedientia and *Devotio*. Obedience, with the forefinger of her right hand raised, and Devotion, with her right hand placed against her breast, both belong to the court of the virtue *Justitia*. There are no traditional examples for their depictions. Taddeo Gaddi gave them, following the Franciscan tradition, the attribute of a yoke.

Tobias and *Luke*. Only these two figures of the cycle of half-length male figures with scrolls (or in one case, with a book) are identified by the inscriptions on the scrolls. One quotes *Tobit, 1:6: Pergebat Jerusalem ad templum domini. Thobias*. This sentence refers to the *Presentation of the Virgin in the Temple* and possibly, at the same time also to the relief of Obedience at Tobias's left. On the other figure's scroll is written: *Cum esset desponsata mater Jesu Maria Joseph. Lucas*. This sentence is not from St. Luke, as Orcagna incorrectly ascribes, but rather from St. Matthew (1:18); the corresponding sentence in St. Luke (1:27) reads: *Ad virginem desponsata viro, cui nomen erat Joseph*. However, the figure should be known by the name given to it by Orcagna. What is important is that the evangelist is alluding to the *Marriage of the Virgin*, the relief to his direct right.

THE RELIEFS ON THE SOUTHWESTERN CORNER PIER

In the center of the five reliefs with half-length figures on the socle area of this corner pier stands the Cardinal Virtue *Fortitudo* (Fortitude), flanked by *Patientia* (Patience) and *Perseverantia* (Perseverance). Adjoining these, as on the other piers, are two reliefs of half-length bearded male figures, pointing to the neighboring scenes of the Life of Mary.

Fortitudo. As a Cardinal Virtue, *Fortitudo* wears a crown on her elaborately waved hair. She wears armor, and a cloak. In her left hand she holds a shield marked with a cross, which in Florence is directly associated with the *Croce del Popolo*. Her right arm embraces a column. Armor and shield illustrate the warlike power of this virtue, whose physical strength is the consequence of her moral force. Her impressive head of hair and the attribute of the column allude to the story of Samson. In this case, Orcagna did not follow the examples set by Andrea Pisano, Taddeo Gaddi, or the campanile of the cathedral of Florence.

Patientia and *Perseverantia*. For these virtues there are no previous examples, not even in the virtue cycle created by Taddeo Gaddi. *Patientia* is depicted as a woman, with right arm raised and her left hand posed in a defensive gesture. Under her arm is an unrolled scroll, the end of which she holds in her right hand. *Perseverantia* is in profile. She wears a laurel wreath on her head, a symbol of eternity and immortality.

Prophet and *Patriarch*. Of both half-length male figures on this pier, the bearded one with the diadem in his hair can be only a prophet. The forefinger of his right hand points to his blank scroll, which originally must have had a text painted on it, no doubt referring to the neighboring scene of the *Annunciation*. His pendant on the side of the relief of the *Nativity* presents an open book in both hands, whose text, now effaced, must have referred to that scene. He wears crown-like headgear, and is thus presumably a patriarch.

THE RELIEFS ON THE SOUTHEASTERN CORNER PIER

The last of the four Cardinal Virtues occupies the socle area of the corner of the fourth pier; this also indicates its position in the hierarchy of the virtues. *Temperantia* (Temperance) is flanked by *Humilitas* (Humility) and *Virginitas* (Virginity). They are joined by the half-length figures of two men from the Old Testament, who relate the reliefs on the pier to those of the Life of Mary.

Temperantia. Temperance, as a crowned Cardinal Virtue, is wrapped in a capelike garment lined with fur, with a close row of buttons running down the front; her arms emerge from slits in the cape. Unlike Giotto and Andrea Pisano, who characterized *Temperantia* with a sheathed sword; unlike the sculptor of the campanile's *Temperantia*, who depicted her mixing wine with water; and unlike Taddeo Gaddi, whose *Temperantia* carries a sickle, Orcagna depicted her holding a compass in both hands. This attribute emphasizes the careful, measuring quality of Temperance.

Temperantia seems to have gained considerably in regard as a virtue during the 13th century. The proper measure had always been an esteemed value of chivalry and in the courts. Now, with the revival of Aristotelian ethics, which considered moderation the core of a well conducted life, *Temperantia* gradually came to be identified with *Sapientia*, or Wisdom. Orcagna's attribute of the compass is thus a symbol of the Aristotelian golden mean.

Humilitas and *Virginitas*. Both of these virtues are ancillary to *Temperantia*, because they embody moderation. Without their names on the scrolls, they would still be identifiable, since they both appear in traditional forms. *Humilitas* appears as a woman clothed in a cape with a cowl, fastened with a clasp. *Virginitas* wears a simple, long-sleeved garment, belted with a length of coarse cord.

Prophet or Apostle and *Patriarch or Priest*. It is difficult to identify the half-length figure next to *Humilitas*, or even to tell whether or not this is a figure from the Old or New Testament. One can only assume that this prophet or apostle was originally identified by the inscription on his scroll, which is blank today. He undoubtedly alluded to the *Epiphany* shown in the adjacent relief of the Life of Mary. On the other side, next to *Virginitas*, is the half-length figure of a bearded man whose hand is posed eloquently on his mouth. He wears crown-like headgear, indicating that he may be a patriarch or a priest of the Old Testament. His gesture could indicate that this man, like Zacharias, has unexpectedly lost his voice; it can also be assumed that his inscription referred to the *Presentation of Christ in the Temple*, which is shown in the next relief.

THE PROPHET UNDER THE RELIEF OF THE DEATH AND ASSUMPTION OF THE VIRGIN

On the piers of the tabernacle's arches, directly over the socle area, are powerfully built bases. Between those of the rear arch, there is a marble block supporting the relief of the *Death and Assumption of the Virgin*. In the center is a relief of a prophet, who is not identifiable, pointing with his right hand to the scenes of the Marian cycle directly above. He belongs to the cycle of the Old and New Testament figures on the socle, and is meant to represent one who prophesied or related the events taking place above him. On either side of the prophet are identical reliefs. In the middle of each sits a cross-legged man wearing a distinctive high hat. Each holds in his arms two symmetrically growing tendrils, whose stems seem to be springing from his body, and whose foliage fills the left and right portions of the diagonally square field of the relief; at the end of each tendril is the face of a child. Perhaps these figures allude to the Tree of Jesse, but this is by no means certain. As of now, the significance of these decorative reliefs remains unresolved.

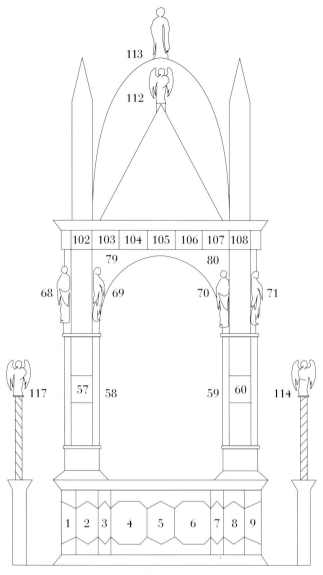

Left (North Side)

Front (West Side)

SCHEMATICS OF TABERNACLE

1. *Prudentia* (Prudence)
2. *Solertia* (Ingenuity)
3. Prophet
4. The Birth of the Virgin
5. *Fides* (Faith)
6. The Presentation of the Virgin in the Temple
7. Tobias
8. *Oboedientia* (Obedience)
9. *Justitia* (Justice)
10. *Devotio* (Devotion)
11. Luke
12. Marriage of the Virgin
13. *Spes* (Hope)
14. Annunciation
15. Prophet
16. *Patientia* (Patience)
17. *Fortitudo* (Fortitude)
18. *Perseverantia* (Perseverance)
19. King
20. Nativity
21. *Caritas* (Love or Charity)
22. Adoration of the Magi
23. Prophet
24. *Humilitas* (Humility)
25. *Temperantia* (Temperance)
26. *Virginitas* (Virginity)

27. Prophet
28. Presentation of Christ in the Temple
29. Annunciation of the Death of the Virgin
30. Prophet
31. *Docilitas* (Erudition)
32. Man with two tendrils
33. Man with two tendrils
34. Prophet
35. The Death of the Virgin
36. The Assumption of the Virgin
37. Angel with violin
38. Angel with psalter
39. Singing angel with lily
40. Singing angel with lily
41. Angel with cymbal
42. Angel with cymbal
43. Seraph
44. Seraph
45. Angel
46. Angel
47. Angel with hands held in prayer
48. Angel with left hand over breast
49. Angel with arms crossed over breast (with stola)
50. Angel with hands held in prayer
51. Angel with arms crossed over breast (profile)
52. Angel with arms crossed over breast (front)
53. Angel with arms crossed over breast (with stola)
54. Angel in cuirass with shield and cudgel

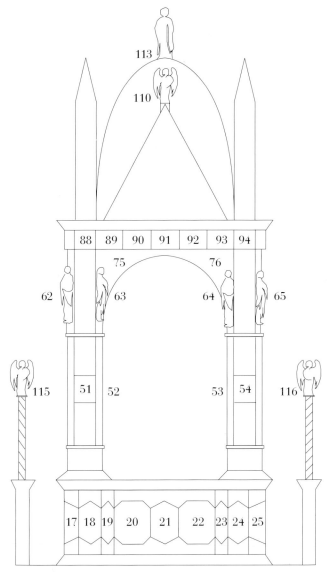

Right (South Side)

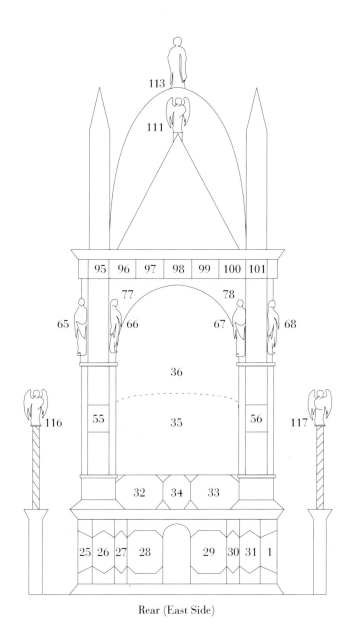

Rear (East Side)

55.	Angel in cuirass with shield and cudgel	
56.	Angel with sheaf and cornucopia	
57.	Angel with sheaf and cornucopia	
58.	Angel with arms crossed over breast (front)	
59.	Angel with right hand over breast	
60.	Angel with arms crossed over breast (profile)	
61.	Peter	
62.	Andrew	
63.	James the Greater	
64.	John	
65.	Thomas	
66.	James the Less	
67.	Philip	
68.	Bartholomew	
69.	Matthew	
70.	Simon	
71.	Thaddeus	
72.	Matthias	
73–80.	Cherubs	
81.	Angel with lily	
82.	Abraham and Isaac	
83.	Angel in cuirass	
84.	Christ's ancestor	
85.	Angel	
86.	Christ's ancestor	
87.	Angel with lily	
88.	Christ's ancestor	
89.	Angel with scroll	

90.	Solomon (?)
91.	Angel
92.	Christ's ancestor
93.	Angel
94.	Christ's ancestor
95.	Angel
96.	Noah
97.	Angel with palm branch
98.	David
99.	Angel with shield
100.	Christ's ancestor
101.	Angel
102.	Christ's ancestor
103.	Angel with messenger's staff
104.	Christ's ancestor
105.	Angel
106.	Christ's ancestor
107.	Angel
108.	Christ's ancestor
109.	Angel (AVE MARIA)
110.	Angel (GRATIA PLENA)
111.	Angel (AVE MARIA)
112.	Angel (GRATIA PLENA)
113.	Michael
114.	Angel with candelabrum
115.	Angel with candelabrum
116.	Angel with candelabrum
117.	Angel with candelabrum

SELECTED BIBLIOGRAPHY

Antal, Frederick. *Florentine Painting and Its Social Background.* London: Kegan Paul, 1948.

Boskovits, Miklos, "Orcagna in 1357—And in Other Times," in *Burlington Magazine* CXIII, no. 818 (May 1971): 239–251.

Cassidy, Brendan, "The Assumption of the Virgin on the Tabernacle of Orsanmichele," in *Journal of the Warburg and Courtauld Institutes* LI (1988): 174–180.

De Wald, Ernest T. *Italian Painting 1200–1600.* New York: Holt, Rinehart and Winston, 1962.

Fabbri, Nancy Rash, and Nina Rutenburg, "The Tabernacle of Orsanmichele in Context," in *The Art Bulletin* LXIII (1981): 385–405.

Ghiberti, Lorenzo. *I Commentarii.* O. Morisani, ed. Naples: Ricciardi, 1947.

Gronau, Hans D. *Andrea Orcagna und Nardo di Cione.* Berlin: Deutscher Kunstverlag, 1937.

Hills, Paul. *The Light of Early Italian Painting.* New Haven: Yale University Press, 1987.

Marle, Raimond van. *The Development of the Italian Schools of Painting,* vol. III. The Hague: Nijhoff, 1924.

Meiss, Millard. *Painting in Florence and Siena after the Black Death.* Princeton: Princeton University Press, 1951.

Offner, Richard. *A Critical and Historical Corpus of Florentine Painting,* Section IV, vol. I, "Andrea di Cione." New York: New York University Press, 1960.

Richa, Giuseppe. *Notizie Istoriche delle Chiese Fiorentine divise ne' suoi Quartieri,* vol. I. Florence, 1754.

Salvini, Roberto, "La Pala Strozzi in Santa Maria Novella," in *L'Arte* XL (1937): 16–45.

Siren, Osvald. *Giotto and Some of His Followers,* vol. I. Cambridge, Mass.: Harvard University Press, 1917.

Smart, Alastair. *The Dawn of Italian Painting 1250–1400.* Ithaca: Cornell University Press, 1978.

Steinweg, Klara. *Andrea Orcagna.* Strasbourg: J.H.E. Heitz, 1929.

Valentiner, Wilhelm R., "Orcagna and the Black Death of 1348," in *The Art Quarterly* XIII (1949): 48–73; 112–128.

Vasari, Giorgio. *Lives of the Most Eminent Painters, Sculptors and Architects,* vol. I. G. De Vere, trans. London: P. L. Ward, 1912.

INDEX

DATE DUE